SbaC

D0845248

YVESTOWN IN THE KITCHEN

A BOOK ABOUT FOOD AND LIVING IN THE KITCHEN

Yvonne Eijkenduijn

www.yvestown.com

PETER PAUPER PRESS, INC.
White Plains, New York

Concept, text, food styling, and photography
YVONNE EIJKENDUIJN
www.yvestown.com

Design and layout
ROEL VAESSEN
www.roelvaessen.com

First published in the Netherlands under the title *Yvestown in de Keuken* by Yvonne Eijkenduijn
Yvestown copyright © text and photography by Yvonne Eijkenduijn,
design by Roel Vaessen
Original edition copyright © 2014 Uitgeverij Snor, Utrecht, Netherlands, *www.uitgeverijsnor.nl*
The rights to this book have been negotiated by Sea of Stories Literary Agency, *www.seaofstories.com*
English translation copyright © 2015 Peter Pauper Press, Inc. English edition co-translated and edited by Sarah Gehrke.
First published in the United States in 2015 by Peter Pauper Press, Inc.

All rights reserved. No part of this book may be used or
reproduced in any manner whatsoever without written
permission from the publisher.
First English edition 2015

Published by Peter Pauper Press, Inc.
202 Mamaroneck Avenue
White Plains, New York 10601
U.S.A.

Library of Congress Cataloging-in-Publication Data

Eijkenduijn, Yvonne.
[Yvestown in de Keuken. English]
Yvestown in the kitchen : a book about food and living in the kitchen / Yvonne Eijkenduijn. -- First English edition.
pages cm
Translation of: Yvestown in de keuken.
Includes index.
ISBN 978-1-4413-1733-9 (hardcover : alk. paper) 1. Kitchens--Pictorial works. 2. Eijkenduijn, Yvonne--Homes and haunts.
3. Food writers--Belgium. 4. Cooking. I. Title.
TX653.E38513 2015
641.5--dc23
2014032030

ISBN 978-1-4413-1733-9
MANUFACTURED FOR
PETER PAUPER PRESS, INC.
PRINTED IN HONG KONG

7 6 5 4 3 2 1

Visit us at *www.peterpauper.com*

For Ben

TABLE OF CONTENTS

INTRODUCTION

As a blogger and online magazine creator, I have unlimited online space at my disposal that I can use to try to inspire people from all over the world. "So why this book?" people kept asking me during the months I was working on it. There's a simple answer to that question: this book is personal, you can hold it in your hands, it is *my book*. Even if my website got hacked or an online virus broke out, this book would still be there. Furthermore, I love books. As a child, I often found it hard to return them to the library. Not because I was lazy, but because my life had become entangled with the protagonists' lives. I couldn't detach myself from them and therefore I wanted to keep the book and its characters near me at all times. I still have that. There are books in my bookcase, and books always come along with me in my bag, too.

Hence my first book, *Yvestown in the Kitchen*. It's about my single biggest passion: food. I love absolutely anything that has to do with food. I love farmers' markets, supermarkets, shopping bags, pretty packaging, and the kitchens where the food is prepared. It would be impossible for me to write a cookbook that only contained recipes. Because I think that the love of food is not only a love of cooking, but also a love for the kitchens the food is prepared in.

The families and friends that are featured in this book are all lovers of good food. They're "foodies." I can honestly say that there are very few people in my life who do not care about food. Cooking and eating have held my longest friendships together. The way to someone's heart really is through their stomach.

So in this book, I visit my friends and family members in their kitchens. The recipes are either their own or I've written them for them. Either way, they have all been tried and tasted by me. I traveled far and wide in search of special ingredients, I washed the dishes countless times, and I gained 17 pounds, but I enjoyed every single moment of it because it meant I could occupy myself with food all day. And, almost as importantly: I could make full use of my considerable collection of shopping bags.

I hope this is the kind of book that's used time and time again—not only as a cookbook, but also as a source of creativity. A nosy glimpse into someone else's kitchen can be incredibly inspiring.

Yvonne Eijkenduijn

MY PANTRY

DAIRY
Organic unsalted butter
Low-fat margarine
Organic low-fat milk
Organic yogurt

OIL
Extra virgin olive oil
Organic sunflower oil
Royal Green extra virgin coconut oil

SALT AND PEPPER
Ground black pepper
Coarse and fine sea salt
Fleur de Sel

CHOCOLATE
Organic extra dark chocolate (at least 80% cocoa)
Organic cocoa powder

HERBS AND SPICES
I buy my herbs and spices online if I can't find them locally.

FRUITS AND VEGETABLES
Plant a vegetable garden if you have the space for it or rent an allotment. Vegetables can be easily grown in pots and planters on a balcony. Visit local farmers' markets. Eat what the seasons bring and eat local produce and organic whenever possible.

EGGS
Use only organic eggs or raise chickens. Chickens don't need a lot of space—about 21 feet per hen. They are great recyclers; one chicken eats an average of 10 pounds of organic waste per year, and lays an egg a day. For more information about raising chickens I recommend *Keeping Chickens*, by Ashley English.

MEAT AND FISH
I'm not a vegetarian, but I try to eat as little meat as possible because it's better for the environment and myself. I buy my fish at the market, and my meat at an organic butcher's. I buy big quantities at once so I can freeze as much as possible.

KITCHENS AND RECIPES

. . . .

. . . .

- meat
- chicken
- fish
- vegetarian
- sweet
- ▶ video instructions: *www.yvestown.com/videos-kitchen*

YVONNE & BORIS

YVONNE & BORIS

I share my kitchen with my husband, Boris, and our cat, BooBoo. Boris owns and runs an advertising and interior assembly company and I write and photograph for my blog *Yvestown* and for various Dutch, British, and US-American interior, food, and lifestyle magazines.

Our house was built in 1896 as a brewer's home (the brewery next door has since burned down). It's located in the north of Belgium, close to the Dutch border.

THE KITCHEN

Our kitchen is located in an extension of the house, jutting out, as it were, right into the garden. You enter the kitchen through one of two pairs of French doors; one pair is at the side of the kitchen and the other at the back, where the pantry is. Two small steps up lead to the adjacent dining room.

Through the kitchen you reach the pantry where Boris has built a large cupboard from reclaimed doors in order to compensate for the lack of storage in the kitchen. We store our food there but also use it as a cloakroom and broom closet.

The kitchen is painted white, with *Cath Kidston* wallpaper on some walls. The wallpaper gives color to the room. I chose a blue *Smeg* fridge as a contrast to all the white surfaces; I also painted the door to the powder room blue. I use pink, red, blue, and green and never deviate from this color palette. My style is a mix of modern and vintage, influenced by Scandinavian and English country house styles.

Boris is the builder and I am the creative mind as well as the painter and decorator. This way we complement each other perfectly. Boris has made the frame of the kitchen island from wood and used a zinc-coated door for the worktop, which is now the ideal surface for rolling out dough and provides extra workspace in general. We sometimes eat a sandwich at the kitchen island, or guests hang out there while I am cooking.

Boris and I keep the mealtimes of a hobbit: breakfast—second breakfast—elevenses—luncheon—afternoon tea—dinner—supper. We love delicious and healthy food shared with a lot of people or just between the two of us.

www.yvestown.com

YVONNE'S FAVORITE SALAD

SERVES 4

INGREDIENTS

- 6 UNPEELED BEETS
- 1 TABLESPOON OLIVE OIL,
  PLUS MORE FOR DRIZZLING
- SALT AND PEPPER
- 4 FIGS
- 2 4-OUNCE BAGS PREWASHED
  MIXED GREENS
- ½ CUP BLUE STILTON

PREPARATION

Preheat the oven to 400°F. Quarter the beets and place them in a medium-sized baking dish. Pour 1 tablespoon of olive oil over the beets and sprinkle them generously with salt and pepper. Roast the beets for 15 to 20 minutes in the oven. Cut the figs into quarters. Remove the dish from the oven, add the figs, and roast for 8 to 10 more minutes, or until the beets are tender. Remove from the oven.

Arrange the mixed greens on a serving plate. Add the beets and figs on top and crumble the Blue Stilton over the salad. Drizzle with olive oil and sprinkle with fresh ground pepper, to taste. Serve with bread.

ZUCCHINI SOUP

SERVES 4

INGREDIENTS

2 LARGE ZUCCHINIS (OR 5 SMALL)
1 BUNCH FRESH CILANTRO
1 RED CHILI PEPPER
3 TABLESPOONS OLIVE OIL
1 TEASPOON SEA SALT
1 TABLESPOON TURMERIC
1 CUP COCONUT MILK
½ CUP WATER
⅔ CUP (ABOUT ⅓ POUND)
  PRE-COOKED AND PEELED
  DUTCH (OR BROWN) SHRIMP

PREPARATION

Cut the zucchini into chunks and place into a large pot. Chop the cilantro and red chili pepper and add them to the pot, along with the olive oil and sea salt. Cover and place over low heat and cook until the zucchini is soft, stirring occasionally. Add the turmeric and stir well. Then remove from heat and puree the contents of the pot with a hand mixer (or carefully pour contents into a regular blender). Add the coconut milk and water and continue to blend until smooth. Serve with the Dutch shrimp on top.

Tip
For a spicier soup, leave some, or all, of the seeds of the red chili pepper in the soup.

Tip
It's also delicious to serve the soup with leek sprouts (sometimes found at specialty stores or farmers' markets).

SURINAMESE CHICKEN PIES

MAKES 10 PIES

INGREDIENTS

2 FREE-RANGE CHICKEN BREASTS
(ABOUT 7 OUNCES EACH)
SALT AND PEPPER
2 TO 2½ CUPS MEDIUM CARROTS,
THINLY SLICED
2½ CUPS FROZEN PEAS
1 TABLESPOON OLIVE OIL
1 RED ONION, CHOPPED
2 CLOVES OF GARLIC, FINELY
CHOPPED
2 TOMATOES, SEEDED AND CHOPPED
3 TO 3½ TABLESPOONS CAPERS
HANDFUL OF FLAT-LEAF PARSLEY,
CHOPPED
5 PUFF PASTRY SHEETS
2 HARD-BOILED EGGS
1 EGG, BEATEN

PREPARATION

Preheat the oven to 400°F. Cover the bottom of a large frying pan or skillet pan with a layer of water and bring it to a boil. Sprinkle the chicken with salt and pepper and add it to the pan, cooking it until almost all of the water is evaporated and the chicken is cooked through. Then remove from heat, cover, and set aside.

Fill a medium pot with water and bring to a boil over high heat. Add the carrots and peas and cook until tender. Drain and set aside.

Remove the chicken breasts from the pan and cut them into small pieces and set aside. Then heat the olive oil in a large frying pan over medium heat. Add the onion, garlic, tomatoes, and chicken to the pan and sauté for 1 to 2 minutes. Stir in the carrots and peas and sauté for another 1 to 2 minutes.

Remove the pan from the heat and mix in the capers and chopped parsley.

Set 10 small disposable aluminum pie pans (about 2 inches wide) on a baking sheet. Carefully unfold the thawed puff pastry sheets and roll them out on a lightly floured surface. Cut the puff pastry sheets into squares to line each pan, making sure there is enough to fold over onto the tops. Then line each of the pans with the pastry and fill them up to the top with the vegetable and chicken mixture. Cut the boiled eggs into thin slices and place 2 slices on top of each pan. Then carefully close the pie by folding up the pastry so that the tips meet each other.

Brush the tops with the beaten egg for a golden brown result. Bake 25 to 30 minutes.

PIECE OF CAKE

YVONNE & BORIS

VICTORIAN SPONGE CAKE

MAKES 1 8-INCH DOUBLE-LAYER
CAKE

INGREDIENTS

1 CUP UNSALTED BUTTER
1¾ CUPS LIGHT BROWN SUGAR
4 EGGS
1 TEASPOON VANILLA EXTRACT
1¾ CUPS SELF-RISING FLOUR
1 TEASPOON BAKING POWDER
PINCH OF SALT
DASH OF MILK

For the filling:
1 TABLESPOON STRAWBERRY JAM
½ POUND OF FRESH STRAWBERRIES,
  SLICED
½ CUP UNSALTED BUTTER, ROOM
  TEMPERATURE
¼ CUP 2% REDUCED-FAT MILK
1 TEASPOON VANILLA EXTRACT
4 CUPS POWDERED SUGAR, PLUS
  MORE FOR GARNISH

PREPARATION

Preheat the oven to 350°F. Butter the bottom and sides of two 8-inch round pans. In a medium bowl, beat the butter and light brown sugar on medium speed until smooth.

Add the eggs and vanilla extract and mix. Stir in the flour, baking powder, and salt just until combined. Do not over-mix! Stir in a dash of milk to thin the batter a bit. Divide the batter between the two pans and bake for 20 to 25 minutes. The cakes are done when a toothpick inserted in the center comes out clean. Allow the cakes to cool for about 5 minutes and then carefully remove them from the pans. Set aside.

Place one of the cakes on your serving plate, and apply a layer of strawberry jam on top. Next layer the strawberries on top of the jam. In a blender or food processor, add the butter, milk, vanilla extract, and powdered sugar and mix until smooth. Flip the other cake upside down on a separate plate so that the flat side is facing up. Spread the filling on top of the cake. Then carefully place the second cake, with the filling side facing down, on top of the first cake, so that the jam and filling are sandwiched together. Sprinkle the top of the cake with additional powdered sugar.

FAVORITE SPOT IN THE KITCHEN

The old large fireplace that we've turned into a bookcase, because it's so spacious. Boris has built shelves inside the fireplace, making it a wonderful space for my cookbooks.

. . . .

DAILY SOURCE OF JOY

My *KitchenAid*. I mix, chop, and cut with it; sometimes I even use it for making bread dough, although I prefer to knead the dough with my hands. I also have an ice-cream-maker attachment for it. It's a miracle machine.

. . . .

BEST-KEPT KITCHEN SECRET

When you assign a fixed place to everything and you keep putting things back into their places, your kitchen will never get cluttered or messy.

. . . .

FAVORITE SURPRISING FLAVOR COMBINATION

Dark chocolate with red chili pepper.

. . . .

DELICIOUS SPICES AND HERBS

Smoked paprika, nutmeg, and fresh cilantro.

. . . .

INSPIRATIONS

www.cathkidston.com
www.countryroad.com.au
www.dille-kamille.nl (in Dutch and French only)

. . . .

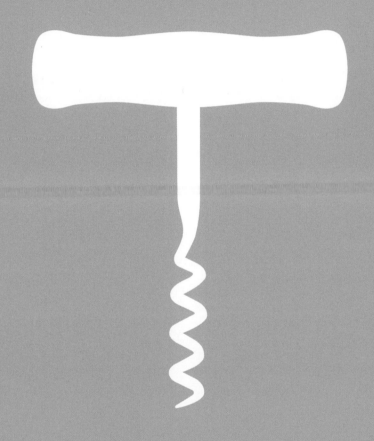

ERIC & PAULIEN

ERIC & PAULIEN

Together Eric and Paulien own and run *Studio Parade*, a multidisciplinary design studio based in 's-Hertogenbosch, a small town in the Netherlands. They are the neighbors of Roel and Ruud *(see page 75)*. Roel, Eric, and Paulien are the creators of the wildly popular modular photo hanging system *ixxi*. Eric and Paulien live with their daughters Rose and Sara and their dog Max.

THE KITCHEN

You enter Eric and Paulien's kitchen through tall sliding doors. The kitchen was a garage when Eric and Paulien bought the home, and two garage doors still give access to the street.

The kitchen is all black, gray, and white. And even though I normally love a lot of cheerful colors, in this case, the monochrome color palette doesn't bore me at all. I love the beautiful staircase that connects the kitchen with the second-floor living room, and the way the light comes in through four windows and is reflected in the 19-feet-long stone countertop.

The kitchen is equipped with the couple's own designs, such as the *Tom* dining chairs, dining table *Phill* and stacking cupboard *Babel*. On the wall behind the dining table hangs an *ixxi* system with pictures of antique china plates from Amsterdam's Rijksmuseum; a boost of color for the kitchen. The Dutch theme, which plays a major part in the room, continues with the use of Delft Blue pottery, the *Buffer Lights* by Dutch designer *Wieki Somers* above the dining table, and a reproduction of Vermeer's *Girl with a Pearl Earring*. Eric and Paulien's kitchen is a real haven of Dutch design.

Eric and Paulien love to drink and eat with friends and with their daughters. They love a good glass of wine with cheese or chocolate. For the rest, they are not up for too much fuss—something that is reflected in their designs, which are pure and honest.

www.studioparade.nl (in Dutch only)
www.ixxidesign.com/en/

N 30 MINUTEN   KOSMOS

CARNIVORIA

PIET HEIN EEK

donna hay   Seizoenskookboek

ERIC & PAULIEN   met The Naked Chef

JOHN JULIUS NORWICH   DE ZEVENTIG BEROEMDST
STEDEN VAN DE WERELD

HET KOOKBOEK

STEAK SANDWICH

SERVES 4

INGREDIENTS

1 TEASPOON GROUND CORIANDER

1 TABLESPOON GROUND CUMIN

ZEST OF 1 ORANGE

1½ TEASPOONS DRIED CHILI FLAKES

3 TABLESPOONS OLIVE OIL, DIVIDED

SALT AND PEPPER

14 OUNCES BRISKET OR SHANK
   STEAK

1 CIABATTA LOAF OR BAGUETTE

2½ CUPS ARUGULA

For the dressing:

3 SPRIGS FRESH MINT, FINELY
   CHOPPED

1 CUP YOGURT

JUICE OF ½ LEMON

1 TEASPOON HONEY

1 TABLESPOON OLIVE OIL

PREPARATION

In a deep plate or bowl, mix the coriander, cumin, orange zest, chili flakes, 2 tablespoons of olive oil, salt, and pepper. Coat both sides of the steak in the marinade and allow to stand for 15 minutes.

Heat 1 tablespoon of olive oil in a frying pan over high heat. Add the steak and fry briefly on both sides until brown. Remove from heat and let the steak rest in the pan while you prepare the dressing.

In a small bowl combine the dressing ingredients and stir together. Then remove the steak from the pan and cut into thin strips. Cut the ciabatta loaf lengthwise and layer one side with the arugula. Pour some of the dressing over the arugula. Place the steak strips on top. Pour more dressing over the steak and cover with the other half of the loaf. Cut into sandwich-sized servings.

ROASTED FENNEL WITH CROUTONS

SERVES 4

INGREDIENTS

1 WHOLE-WHEAT CIABATTA ROLL

1 WHITE CIABATTA ROLL

5 TABLESPOONS OLIVE OIL, DIVIDED

2 FENNEL BULBS

2 TABLESPOONS UNSALTED BUTTER

$1/3$ CUP WATER

½ BUNCH FLAT-LEAF PARSLEY,
  COARSELY CHOPPED

2 SPRIGS FRESH THYME

5 ANCHOVY FILLETS

SALT AND PEPPER

PREPARATION

Preheat the oven to 400°F. Tear the ciabatta rolls into pieces and put them on a baking tray. Toss them with 3 tablespoons of olive oil and bake for 5 minutes. Remove from the oven and set aside.

Cut the fennel lengthwise and then cut each half into quarters. Heat a skillet over high heat, and add 2 tablespoons of olive oil. Add the fennel to the pan and fry until browned on both sides. Then add the butter and water and cook for about 5 minutes. Remove from the heat.

Put the fennel with its cooking liquid in a large baking dish and sprinkle with the parsley and thyme leaves. Lay the anchovies and ciabatta croutons on top, drizzle with a little olive oil and salt and pepper to taste. Bake for 25 minutes.

CHOCOLATE MARBLE CAKE

MAKES 1 9-INCH DOUBLE-LAYER CAKE

INGREDIENTS

½ CUP COCOA POWDER
½ CUP WATER
2¼ CUPS LIGHT BROWN SUGAR, DIVIDED
1⅓ CUPS UNSALTED BUTTER
2 TEASPOONS VANILLA EXTRACT
5 EGGS
½ TEASPOON SALT
2 TEASPOONS BAKING POWDER
½ CUP MILK
3 CUPS ALL-PURPOSE WHEAT FLOUR

For the icing:
11 OUNCES MILK CHOCOLATE
⅓ CUP WHIPPED CREAM
2 TABLESPOONS UNSALTED BUTTER
½ TEASPOON VANILLA EXTRACT

PREPARATION

Preheat the oven to 350°F. Generously butter the bottom and sides of two 9-inch round pans and set aside.

In a medium bowl, whisk together the cocoa powder, water, and ½ cup of the sugar and set aside.

Melt the butter in a small saucepan over low heat. Then mix the melted butter with the remaining light brown sugar in a large mixing bowl, until the mixture is smooth. Add the vanilla extract and eggs (one at a time) and mix until well combined. Then add the salt and baking powder and mix. Alternately add the milk and flour in small parts until well blended.

Spoon 1⅔ cups of the vanilla batter into the bowl with the cocoa powder, water, and light brown sugar mixture and combine until smooth. Divide the vanilla batter and chocolate batter each evenly into two separate bowls (you should have two bowls of vanilla, and two bowls of chocolate).

Set aside one bowl of vanilla, one bowl of chocolate, and one of the cake pans. With the other bowls and pan, cover the bottom of the first cake pan with a layer of vanilla batter. Next, spoon a few large dollops of chocolate batter on top of the vanilla batter and spread evenly. Repeat with alternating vanilla and chocolate layers until you have used up all the batter. Then repeat this process to fill the second cake pan with the batter from the two remaining bowls.

Bake the cakes for 55 minutes. Remove from the oven and set aside until completely cooled down. Carefully remove them from the pans and place them on a large sheet tray or on plates.

For the icing:
Melt the chocolate in a small saucepan over low heat, stirring constantly. Remove from heat and let cool. Then mix in the other icing ingredients and stir until smooth. Spread a layer of icing on top of one of the cakes. Then carefully place the other cake on top of the first. Frost the top and sides of the cake with the remaining icing.

FAVORITE SPOT IN THE KITCHEN

Paulien's favorite spot is sitting on a chair while she is watching Eric cook. In the meantime the girls like to hang out perched atop the long countertop.

DAILY SOURCE OF JOY

Eric standing behind the counter: he is the cook in the house. Paulien loves to chat with him while he prepares food for the rest of the family.

BEST-KEPT CULINARY SECRET

Eric's coffee-making techniques. And they shall remain a secret! He makes the best coffee in town, and that has nothing to do with the espresso machine and everything with the man that serves the coffee.

FAVORITE SURPRISING FLAVOR COMBINATION

Caramelized fennel.

FAVORITE SPICES AND HERBS

Garlic and fennel seeds.

INSPIRATIONS

www.ibride.fr
www.muuto.com

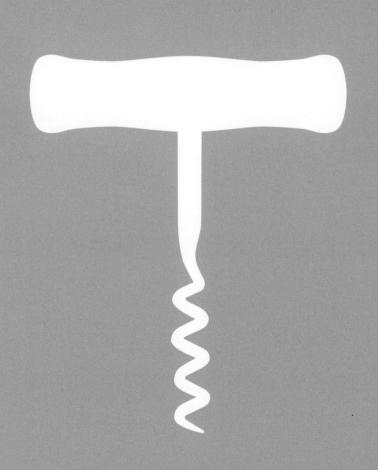

MARIANNE & HARRY

MARIANNE & HARRY

Marianne and Harry live in the ground-floor apartment of an old, typically Dutch house in the old town center of 's-Hertogenbosch in the Netherlands. Their daughter Sarah and her daughter live in the apartment above.

When the building behind the house went up for sale, their son Wim took up residence there. He now lives on the second floor and runs a shop with Sarah on the ground floor. Their shop *Vintage Room* sells both old and new interior decoration, such as *Jieldé* lamps and *Tolix* chairs.

Marianne and Harry share their kitchen with dogs Marini and Toutuffi and an aviary with lots of birds; and there are regular visits from their son, daughters, and grandchildren.

THE KITCHEN

When I come in through the front door and walk through the long hallway toward the partially covered patio area (which serves as a passage between the dining room, the kitchen, and a back room) I become deliriously happy. Marianne and Harry's kitchen reminds me of a small Victorian menagerie complete with birdcages and dogs. In the beautiful green patio, a powdery-pink wrought-iron spiral staircase leads to the upstairs balcony and Sarah's apartment.

It's this indoor/outdoor feel that makes Harry and Marianne's kitchen unique. The glass wall and sliding doors are almost invisible because of all the large potted plants that Marianne has put in front of them. The modern kitchen cabinets don't clash with the style of the old property. Thanks to lots of soft pastel colors and a balanced mix of classic and modern furniture, the kitchen matches the rest of the interior and the architecture of the building perfectly.

There's an array of photos and souvenirs from trips or beautiful moments with their children and grandchildren stuck on the refrigerator door. Love of family radiates through this kitchen. You've arrived in the very heart of the home.

www.vintageroom.nl (in Dutch only)

ROAST ROLLS

INGREDIENTS
5 SCALLIONS
5 MEDIUM CARROTS
SALT AND PEPPER
10 SLICES OF ROAST BEEF (MEDIUM
   TO THIN SANDWICH SLICES)
4 TABLESPOONS OLIVE OIL

For the sauce:
2 TABLESPOONS BROWN SUGAR
3 TABLESPOONS SOY SAUCE
3 TABLESPOONS MIRIN (RICE WINE)

PREPARATION
Finely chop the scallions and put them in a small bowl. Grate the carrots and add them to the bowl. Season with salt and pepper to taste, and mix together. Put a small amount of filling into a slice of roast beef and roll it up. Repeat with the rest of the roast beef slices and set aside.

Heat the oil in a skillet pan over medium-high heat. Fry the roast beef rolls in the pan until brown on all sides.

In a small bowl, combine the sauce ingredients and mix. Serve the rolls with the sauce and rice or prawn crackers.

MARIANNE & HARRY

CHICKEN SATAY WITH CARROT COUSCOUS

SERVES 4

INGREDIENTS

4 SCALLIONS
12 OUNCES BONELESS CHICKEN
   BREASTS
1 TABLESPOON GRATED GINGER
1 TABLESPOON LEMON JUICE
2 TEASPOONS CURRY POWDER
1 TEASPOON SOY SAUCE
1 TEASPOON INDONESIAN DARK
   SWEET SOY SAUCE
1 TEASPOON HONEY
SALT AND PEPPER
OLIVE OIL
SKEWERS

For the couscous:
2 CUPS COUSCOUS
2 CUPS WATER
SEA SALT, TO TASTE
2 LARGE CARROTS, GRATED
DASH OF OLIVE OIL
HANDFUL FRESH CILANTRO,
   CHOPPED

PREPARATION

Preheat the oven to 425°F. Chop the scallions and place in a medium bowl. Cut the chicken breasts into cubes and add them to the bowl. Add the ginger, lemon juice, curry powder, soy sauces, and honey. Add salt and pepper to taste. Mix everything together (preferably with your hands) until the chicken is thoroughly coated. Then thread the chicken onto skewers. Grease a medium-sized baking dish lightly with a drizzle of olive oil and place the chicken skewers in it with some distance between them. Cook for about 20 minutes in the oven.

For the couscous:

Into a saucepan, pour the couscous, water, and a pinch of sea salt. Add the carrots on top. Cover and cook over low heat for about 15 minutes, until the couscous has absorbed the water. Then remove from heat and let sit for about 10 minutes. Fluff with a fork and add a dash of olive oil. Sprinkle the cilantro on top and serve with the chicken skewers.

BANANA FRITTERS

INGREDIENTS

2 OVERRIPE BANANAS

2 TABLESPOONS MILK

2 EGGS

1 TABLESPOON UNSALTED BUTTER,
   MELTED

1 CUP ALL-PURPOSE WHEAT FLOUR

¼ CUP SUPERFINE SUGAR

1 TEASPOON BAKING POWDER

½ TEASPOON SALT

¼ TEASPOON GROUND CINNAMON

¼ TEASPOON GROUND NUTMEG

1 QUART SUNFLOWER OIL
   (FOR DEEP-FRYING)

POWDERED SUGAR

PREPARATION

In a medium bowl, mash the bananas with a fork. Add the milk, eggs, and butter and blend until smooth. In a separate bowl, mix together the flour, sugar, baking powder, salt, cinnamon, and nutmeg. Then combine the dry ingredients with the banana mixture.

In a fryer, heat the sunflower oil to 375°F. Using a soup spoon or ice cream scoop, drop a large spoonful or scoop of batter into the oil. Flip when golden and continue to fry until golden on both sides. Remove from the oil and drain on a plate lined with a paper towel. Repeat with the remaining dough.

Sprinkle the banana fritters with powdered sugar.

MARIANNE & HARRY

FAVORITE SPOT IN THE KITCHEN

The beautiful old dining table with a view of the patio.

~~~~~~~~~~~~~~~~~~~~~~~~~~~~

DAILY SOURCE OF JOY

The dishwasher. Because of the shop behind the house, their kitchen kind of serves as a canteen for everyone, yet it is always tidy, because all dirty dishes are put straight into the dishwasher.

~~~~~~~~~~~~~~~~~~~~~~~~~~~~

BEST-KEPT CULINARY SECRET

For a crispy batter for fish or chicken, use semolina instead of flour. You can also dip pineapple slices in semolina and bake them in sunflower oil until golden brown.

~~~~~~~~~~~~~~~~~~~~~~~~~~~~

FAVORITE SURPRISING FLAVOR COMBINATION

Endive-and-potato mash with applesauce and nutmeg.

~~~~~~~~~~~~~~~~~~~~~~~~~~~~

FAVORITE SPICES AND HERBS

Curry, ginger, cinnamon, cloves, and vanilla pods. Lemongrass, galangal, and soto.

~~~~~~~~~~~~~~~~~~~~~~~~~~~~

INSPIRATIONS

www.hayonstudio.com

~~~~~~~~~~~~~~~~~~~~~~~~~~~~

ROEL & RUUD

ROEL & RUUD

Roel and Ruud share their kitchen full-time with their cat Felix and part-time with their son, Ties. Roel is one of the creators of *ixxi*, a modular photo hanging system, which he invented with Eric and Paulien *(see page 37)*.

He's my best friend, an independent graphic designer, and the designer of this book.

THE KITCHEN

Roel and Ruud's ground-floor apartment is located in an apartment complex that was built in 1955. Their home is within walking distance of the old city center of 's-Hertogenbosch in the Netherlands and has a lovely little garden.

When Roel and Ruud first moved in, the house had three small bedrooms, a spacious living room, a bathroom, and a kitchen. They demolished one of the bedroom walls to make the kitchen larger.

The basic kitchen decor, the structural contours of the supporting walls, and the sleek interior design by *Studio Parade* provide a good mix of tough and cute. That makes Roel and Ruud's kitchen a true "big boys" kitchen. *Nina Campbell's* frivolous *Wisteria* wallpaper from the *Fandango* collection lines one wall. But the contrast with the sleek vintage chair and the graphic *Donna Wilson* cushion makes for a bold, graphic, and humorous overall impression. The many colorful book covers on *Studio Parade's* bookcase *Paperback* add a boost of color to the white wall.

Tall French doors lead into the garden, where two chickens provide fresh eggs daily. Chickens in the city? No problem, according to Roel and Ruud. As long as you only raise hens, there's no noise, which keeps the neighbors happy, too.

Roel and Ruud love delicious and healthy food. They like to shop at their local organic farmers' market or at an organic supermarket, and they prefer to get their wine from a proper wine merchant and meat from the local butcher's rather than the supermarket—Roel and Ruud don't mind spending a bit more if they know that the products are good and honest. And beautiful packaging is never a waste either, delighting them whenever they open the fridge.

www.roelvaessen.com
www.ixxidesign.com/en

CLUB SANDWICH WITH CHICKEN AND CRAB

SERVES 4

INGREDIENTS

12 SLICES OF WHOLE GRAIN OR
   SPELT BREAD
1 TABLESPOON OLIVE OIL
6 OUNCES BONELESS CHICKEN
   BREASTS
SALT AND PEPPER
1 CUP PREMADE CRAB SALAD
1 AVOCADO
1 TABLESPOON LIGHT MAYONNAISE
¼ CUP + 2 TABLESPOONS CHOPPED
   CHIVES

PREPARATION

Toast the bread, place three slices on a plate each and set aside.

Rub olive oil onto the chicken and sprinkle with salt and pepper. Grill the chicken in a grill pan and set aside.

Spread crab salad on four slices of toast (make it a nice thick layer). Slice the avocado and layer some slices over the crab salad on each sandwich. Season with salt and pepper, to taste. Spread another thin layer of crab salad over the avocado on each sandwich. Place a slice of toast on top of each and cover with a thin layer of mayonnaise. Sprinkle each with the chopped chives.

Cut the chicken in thin slices and place some on top of the chives for each sandwich. Spread a thin layer of mayonnaise over the remaining slices of toast and place on top of the sandwiches. Cut sandwiches into quarters.

ROEL & RUUD

BUTTERNUT SQUASH RISOTTO

SERVES 4

INGREDIENTS

1 (REGULAR-SIZED) BUTTERNUT
 SQUASH
¾ CUP GRATED PARMESAN
1 CLOVE OF GARLIC, CHOPPED
ZEST OF ½ LEMON
PEPPER
OLIVE OIL
6- TO 7-OUNCE BOX OF MUSHROOM
 RISOTTO
4 SPRIGS FRESH FLAT-LEAF PARSLEY

PREPARATION

Preheat the oven to 400°F. Peel the squash and cut into bite-sized chunks and place them in a large baking dish. Sprinkle the parmesan on top. Add the garlic and lemon zest. Sprinkle with freshly-ground pepper. Add a generous dash of olive oil and cook for about 15 to 20 minutes.

In the meantime, prepare the risotto rice according to the instructions on the package. Make sure there is liquid in the bottom of the pot, or wok, right until the risotto rice is ready.

Serve the risotto topped with the butternut squash and sprinkle with some extra grated parmesan. Garnish with a sprig of parsley.

SPICY PASTA WITH EGGPLANT, RICOTTA AND SALMON

INGREDIENTS

1 CUP RICOTTA (ABOUT 8 OUNCES)

2 MEDIUM EGGPLANTS

SALT

OLIVE OIL

2 CLOVES OF GARLIC, CHOPPED

1 RED ONION, CHOPPED

2 14.5-OUNCE CANS DICED
  TOMATOES

1 TEASPOON CHILI POWDER

9 OUNCES FRESH SPAGHETTI

6 2-OUNCE SALMON STEAKS

FRESHLY-GROUND PEPPER, TO TASTE

FRESH BASIL (ABOUT 6 LEAVES)

PREPARATION

Preheat the oven to 400°F. Cover a baking tray with parchment paper and turn out the ricotta onto the tray. (Pricking small holes in the bottom of the packaging will make it glide out easily.) Place the ricotta in the center of the oven and bake for 15 minutes.

While the ricotta is baking, slice the eggplant length-wise and place the slices in a large baking dish. Sprinkle with salt and a dash of olive oil. After the ricotta has baked for 15 minutes, put the eggplant in the oven next to the ricotta and bake both for another 15 minutes.

While the ricotta and eggplant bake, fill a large pot with water for the spaghetti and place it over high heat to bring up to a boil. Heat about 1 tablespoon of olive oil in a frying pan over medium heat. Add the garlic and onion and cook for a few minutes. Then add the tomatoes and chili powder and stir constantly until nicely blended into a sauce.

Once you have removed the ricotta and eggplant from the oven, cut the eggplant slices into smaller chunks and add to the tomato sauce. Stir and then remove from heat. Cut the ricotta into large chunks and set aside.

By now, your pot of water should be boiling. Cook the spaghetti per the package instructions. While the spaghetti is cooking, season the salmon steaks with salt and pepper, sprinkle with some olive oil, add to a large baking dish, and bake them (uncovered) in the oven for 15 minutes.

To serve, distribute the pasta over individual plates, add the sauce, then the ricotta and finally the salmon steaks on top. Garnish each with a basil leaf.

APPLE AND PEAR CRUMBLE

SERVES 6

INGREDIENTS

2 LARGE APPLES (PINK LADIES WORK
    WELL)

2 PEARS

¼ CUP RAISINS

1 TEASPOON GROUND CINNAMON

1 TEASPOON VANILLA EXTRACT

½ CUP UNSALTED BUTTER

½ CUP SUPERFINE SUGAR

2 CUPS ALL-PURPOSE WHEAT FLOUR

PINCH OF SALT

2 TABLESPOONS MILK

VANILLA ICE CREAM OR LEMON
    SORBET (OPTIONAL)

PREPARATION

Preheat the oven to 400°F. Cut the apples and pears into chunks (they don't need to be peeled). Place them in a medium-sized baking dish and toss with the raisins, cinnamon, and vanilla extract. Set aside.

Using your hands, mix the butter, sugar, flour, and salt in a medium bowl until the mixture gets crumbly. Add one tablespoon of milk and continue to mix—the lumps should become thick and firm. If needed, add another tablespoon of milk. Spread the mixture evenly over the apples and pears. Bake for 30 to 35 minutes.

Serve with a scoop of vanilla ice cream or lemon sorbet (optional).

FAVORITE SPOT IN THE KITCHEN

The armchair in the corner of the room, over-looking the garden. It's the perfect place to be, especially in springtime and with the French doors open.

DAILY SOURCE OF JOY

The *Solis* espresso machine for a daily fresh cup of coffee at breakfast.

BEST-KEPT CULINARY SECRET

For a perfectly cooked egg, first boil water in a kettle. Pour the boiling water into a saucepan and carefully lower the eggs into the water with a spoon. Boil the eggs for 6 minutes to get them perfectly soft and tasty.

FAVORITE SURPRISING FLAVOR COMBINATION

Ice cream with a splash of good olive oil is very tasty.

FAVORITE SPICES AND HERBS

Mustard, cinnamon, fresh mint, and rosemary.

INSPIRATIONS

www.donnahay.com
www.ztrdg.nl (in Dutch only)

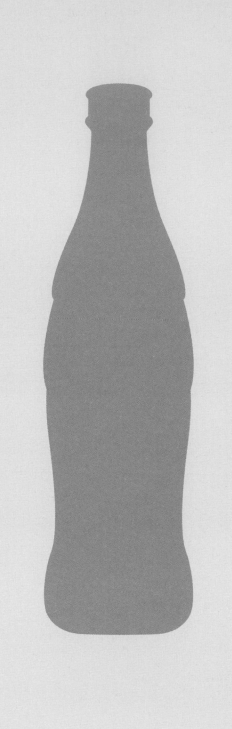

KARINE & STEVE

KARINE & STEVE

Karine is a French blogger friend of mine. She lives in West London with her husband Steve and their daughter Mila. Karine and her sister Elodie own and run the award-winning online concept store *Bodie and Fou*, which sells home accessories, design, and fashion to many customers worldwide.

THE KITCHEN

It's a typical feature of London's ubiquitous terraced houses that the kitchen is situated at the back of the house. Karine and Steve's kitchen has a glass roof that covers the entire width of the house, which makes it spacious and light. But there were, and still are, more adjustments to be made to get the kitchen to properly reflect Karine's taste and style. She has already painted the cabinets black, and shortly they will install a new counter and worktop and substitute the stone floor with seamless resin flooring.

Karine's style is simple, practical, and authentic. Many things in Karine's home are also for sale at *Bodie and Fou*. It's a "rockstar look" that she's going for: lots of wood, leather, and linen. It has to look cool and be bold. There are simple black-and-white ceramics by designer *Nelson Sepuvelda*, old industrial shelves and rustic tables and cabinets. This might sound pretty macho, but Karine and Steve's kitchen actually looks very feminine to me. There are inspirational black-and-white photographs all over the place, simply stuck onto the wall with bits of tape. On the refrigerator are photos of Steve and Mila.

The adjacent green courtyard provides space for barbecues and cozy dinner parties. Because that's what Steve and Karine really like doing: having dinner with friends and their friends' children. Everyone is welcome in their kitchen—even the dog.

www.bodieandfou.com
blog.bodieandfou.com

KARINE & STEVE

SPICY SHRIMP SALAD

SERVES 8

INGREDIENTS
½ CUP BULGUR
2 CUPS OF BOILING WATER
1 SCALLION
1 AVOCADO
7 OUNCES LARGE SHRIMP, BOILED
    AND PEELED
5 TABLESPOONS OLIVE OIL, DIVIDED
JUICE OF ½ LEMON
2 TABLESPOONS SWEET CHILI SAUCE
½ TEASPOON GROUND CUMIN
HANDFUL OF FRESH CILANTRO,
    CHOPPED

PREPARATION
Place the bulgur in a large bowl and add the boiling water. Cover with a plate until the water has been absorbed. Slice the scallion and cut the avocado into chunks. Place in a large bowl and add the shrimp. Mix in 4 tablespoons of olive oil, the lemon juice, sweet chili sauce, and cumin. Set aside.

Heat 1 tablespoon of olive oil in a frying pan over medium to high heat. Briefly fry the bulgur in the pan until the grains are golden brown. Mix everything in a salad bowl and garnish with the cilantro.

KARINE & STEVE

COCONUT BROWNIES

MAKES 8 BROWNIES

INGREDIENTS
½ CUP UNSALTED BUTTER
5 OUNCES OF DARK CHOCOLATE
2 EGGS
1 CUP LIGHT BROWN SUGAR
2 TEASPOONS VANILLA EXTRACT
1⅓ CUPS ALL-PURPOSE WHEAT FLOUR
1 TABLESPOON COCOA POWDER
⅓ CUP COCONUT FLAKES

PREPARATION
Preheat the oven to 350°F. Melt the butter and the chocolate in a small saucepan over low heat, stirring constantly until fully melted. Remove from heat. Mix in the eggs and the sugar. Then slowly add all the other ingredients, one by one, and stir until combined.

Grease an 8" x 8" baking pan with butter. Pour the mixture in the baking pan and bake for 25 minutes. The brownies are supposed to be sticky and gooey, so take care not to bake it too long. Cut into squares.

KARINE & STEVE

FAVORITE SPOT IN THE KITCHEN

The dining table, where family and friends come together.

===

DAILY SOURCE OF JOY

The fact that Mila can now make the gluten-free pancakes that Karine always used to make for her, and that Karine's mother, in turn, always used to make for Karine and her siblings.

===

BEST-KEPT CULINARY SECRET

The sneaky spoonful of cocoa powder that goes into Mila's vegetable smoothie. That way she drinks her smoothies without any fuss.

===

FAVORITE SURPRISING FLAVOR COMBINATION

Chocolate with coconut.

===

FAVORITE SPICES AND HERBS

Basil, sea salt, and rosemary.

===

INSPIRATIONS

www.thesimplethings.com
www.vosgesparis.com
www.byaprilandmay.com

===

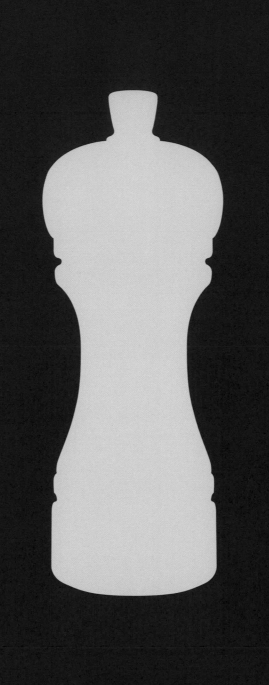

JOSCHA & ERWIN

JOSCHA & ERWIN

Hidden away in a stretch of land reclaimed from the sea in the province of Zeeland (in the south-west of the Netherlands), lies a small hamlet. This is where Joscha, Erwin, and their four children Floyd, Lola Elvis, Roemer, and Pippa Rose live.

Joscha is a blogger friend and one of my girl-trip companions. With a few friends we take regular trips to different cities in Europe. We do something cultural, we shop, and we have dinner, but most of all we bond as women.

Joscha is a creative entrepreneur, a mother, and a stamp maker. On her blog she writes about her work and motherhood.

THE KITCHEN

The original house, built in 1904, was too small to house a family of six. Joscha and Erwin designed an extension built entirely from wood, steel, and glass. As a result, almost the entire ground floor is one large open space, combining living room, play area, office, and kitchen.

The kitchen was designed around their *Siemens* hob (cooktop): there needed to be sufficient space left to build the elevated worktop. Through the narrow hallway in the back of the kitchen you reach the children's bedrooms. Strangely enough I've never been beyond the kitchen—I have never even seen the front of the house. I'm wondering if it actually exists!

Because the space is used for cooking, eating, working, and living in, you will find a large array of odd objects in the kitchen area. Erwin has hung his guitars on the wall next to the *Smeg* fridge and a piano sits next to the *IKEA* dining tables. Joscha and Erwin's kitchen is an organized hodgepodge of pleasantness, with lots of room to cook, eat, and play. It's all about being together, reading books under the pretty *Studio Snowpuppe* light or to just sit and gaze outside, into the polder landscape.

Joscha and Erwin are vegetarians, and the children are slowly (and non-compulsorily) becoming vegetarians, too. Until a while ago, their young son Roemer still felt like having a hot dog sometimes, but he is now completely over it because he feels sorry for the animals.

www.muswerk.nl (in Dutch only)

JOSCHA & ERWIN

CARROT SOUP WITH TIKKA MASALA

SERVES 6

INGREDIENTS

2¼ POUNDS CARROTS
1 TEASPOON COARSE SEA SALT
2 TABLESPOONS OLIVE OIL
2 LARGE WHITE ONIONS
2 CLOVES OF GARLIC
2 TABLESPOONS TIKKA MASALA
   PASTE
¾ CUP COCONUT MILK
2 CUPS WATER
HANDFUL FRESH CILANTRO
1 RED CHILI PEPPER,
   FINELY CHOPPED

PREPARATION

Cut the carrots into large chunks, place them in a skillet pan with the salt and olive oil, cover and cook on low heat until tender, stirring every once in a while.

In the meantime, chop the onions and the garlic and fry them in a frying pan with the tikka masala paste over medium heat until soft. Add the cooked carrots, stir to combine, and remove from the heat. Pour the contents of the frying pan into a blender and mix until smooth. Then pour into a large saucepan and place over medium heat. While reheating the soup, stir in the coconut milk and the water.

Garnish with the cilantro and red chili pepper.

JOSCHA & ERWIN

VEGETARIAN PIZZAS

SERVES 6

INGREDIENTS

4 CUPS ALL-PURPOSE WHEAT FLOUR
1 TEASPOON INSTANT DRY YEAST
1½ TEASPOONS SALT
1⅓ CUPS WARM WATER
1 TABLESPOON CANOLA OIL

For artichoke pizza:
2 TABLESPOONS OLIVE OIL
2 WHITE ONIONS, CHOPPED
2 CLOVES OF GARLIC, CHOPPED
1 14-OUNCE CAN ARTICHOKE HEARTS
1¼ CUPS GORGONZOLA, CRUMBLED
4 SPRIGS OF ROSEMARY (LEAVES
   ONLY)
SALT AND PEPPER, TO TASTE

For spinach pizza:
2 TABLESPOONS OLIVE OIL
2 WHITE ONIONS, CHOPPED
2 CLOVES OF GARLIC, CHOPPED
2½ CUPS (ABOUT 10.5 OUNCES)
   FRESH SPINACH, FINELY CHOPPED
1 CUP GRATED PECORINO

PREPARATION

Mix the flour, yeast, and salt in a bowl. Add the warm water and the canola oil. Knead with your hands for about 5 to 10 minutes, until the dough is smooth. The dough will be very sticky in the beginning, but try not to use too much flour when kneading to make sure the dough stays firm. The dough will become less sticky after about 5 minutes.

Shape into a ball, dust with some flour, place in a bowl and cover the bowl with a moist dish cloth. Set aside for 2 to 3 hours, so the dough can rise. Then dust some flour on your worktop and roll out pizza shapes in your preferred size.

For artichoke pizza:
Preheat the oven to 350°F. Place the pizza base(s) on parchment paper on a baking tray. Heat the olive oil in a frying pan over medium to high heat and add the onions and garlic. Stir and fry over medium heat until soft. Sprinkle the onions and garlic and the rest of the ingredients on the pizza base, salt and pepper to taste, and add a dash of olive oil. Bake for about 25 minutes.

For spinach pizza:
Preheat the oven to 350°F. Place the pizza base(s) on parchment paper on a baking tray. Heat the olive oil in a frying pan over medium to high heat and add the onions and garlic. Stir and fry over medium heat until soft. Add the spinach and fry briefly. Place everything on the pizza base, sprinkle with the pecorino, season with salt and pepper to taste, and add a dash of olive oil. Bake for about 25 minutes.

JOSCHA & ERWIN

STICKY LEMON AND POPPY SEED CUPCAKES

MAKES ABOUT 20 CUPCAKES

INGREDIENTS

1 CUP SUPERFINE SUGAR

½ CUP UNSALTED BUTTER, ROOM
  TEMPERATURE

⅓ CUP SUNFLOWER OIL

ZEST OF 3 LEMONS

4 EGGS

¼ CUP HOT WATER

2 CUPS ALL-PURPOSE WHEAT FLOUR

2 TEASPOONS BAKING POWDER

½ CUP OAT BRAN

3 TABLESPOONS POPPY SEEDS

STICKY BUN SUGAR OR POWDERED
  SUGAR, FOR GARNISHING
  (OPTIONAL)

SPRINKLES FOR GARNISHING
  (OPTIONAL)

For the syrup:

¾ CUP SUPERFINE SUGAR

JUICE OF 3 LEMONS

PREPARATION

Preheat the oven to 350°F. Line 20 cupcake tin cups with paper cupcake liners. In a medium bowl, beat the sugar, butter, oil, and lemon zest until smooth. Beat in the eggs one at a time. Add the hot water and mix until smooth. Slowly add the flour and baking powder. Then add the oat bran and the poppy seeds, and mix until combined.

Pour the batter into the lined cupcake pan, distributing the batter equally (each should be a little more than half-full). Bake for 15 to 20 minutes. In the meantime, for the syrup, add the sugar and lemon juice to a small saucepan. Place over low heat and stir until the sugar is dissolved.

Once you have removed the cupcakes from the oven, prick little holes in the tops with a toothpick. Then carefully pour the warm lemon syrup over the cupcakes. Garnish with sugar and sprinkles (optional).

Tip

These measurements will also yield an entire 7-inch loaf.

FAVORITE SPOT IN THE KITCHEN

The dining table, where the family spends most of the time chatting, drawing, doing homework, working, and eating. In this house nobody ever sits on the couch.

◇◇◇◇◇◇◇◇◇◇◇◇◇◇◇◇◇◇◇◇◇◇◇◇◇◇◇◇◇◇◇◇

DAILY SOURCE OF JOY

They make their daily delicious "slow coffee" with the *Chemex* coffeepot and kettle—using freshly ground beans, of course.

◇◇◇◇◇◇◇◇◇◇◇◇◇◇◇◇◇◇◇◇◇◇◇◇◇◇◇◇◇◇◇◇

BEST-KEPT KITCHEN SECRET

The secret to cleaning a really dirty pan or baking tray is by placing it in a sealed plastic bag with a generous dash of ammonia. Leave this overnight and wash the next day very thoroughly with detergent and hot water. But beware: wear gloves and do not lean over the bag when you open it, as toxic fumes will be released. It's best to do this outside and away from animals and small children.

◇◇◇◇◇◇◇◇◇◇◇◇◇◇◇◇◇◇◇◇◇◇◇◇◇◇◇◇◇◇◇◇

FAVORITE SURPRISING FLAVOR COMBINATION

Dark chocolate with lavender.

◇◇◇◇◇◇◇◇◇◇◇◇◇◇◇◇◇◇◇◇◇◇◇◇◇◇◇◇◇◇◇◇

FAVORITE SPICES AND HERBS

Fresh garlic and ginger.

◇◇◇◇◇◇◇◇◇◇◇◇◇◇◇◇◇◇◇◇◇◇◇◇◇◇◇◇◇◇◇◇

INSPIRATIONS

www.poketo.com

◇◇◇◇◇◇◇◇◇◇◇◇◇◇◇◇◇◇◇◇◇◇◇◇◇◇◇◇◇◇◇◇

WILLEM

WILLEM

The industrial designer Willem lives above his design studio, *Customr*, in Amsterdam. I've known him all my life. He is the son of Auntie Janneke, my mother's friend of more than fifty years.

THE KITCHEN

A steep staircase leads to the hall of Willem's apartment. To the back of the hall is the kitchen with adjacent dining area. At the back, there is a roof terrace, where Willem grows vegetables, herbs, and plants in pots, stretched out over the entire length of the apartment. The kitchen and dining room overlook the backyards, balconies, and facades of the houses of Amsterdam's *Oud Zuid* ("old south"), as the area where Willem lives is called. It always amazes me, a child of the countryside, how peaceful and green this area is. It's an oasis of tranquility in the middle of the city.

Willem's kitchen is sleek, well-organized, and functional. No fuss for him—just the bare essentials for making a daily meal for him alone or for the many friends and family members who frequently come to visit. It is a proper working kitchen, and he feels relaxed here.

The kitchen cabinets are from *IKEA*. Willem designed the polyester countertop himself. The contents of his kitchen drawers reflect his character: organized and tidy. The seamless resin floor runs throughout the apartment.

Willem loves Asian cuisine. He likes to dine, whether he is going out or staying in, and is often found in the local Asian supermarket on the hunt for hard-to-find ingredients. He is a foodie who loves to cook for others and who can talk about food for hours. I know few people who are as passionate about cooking, who make so many "yummy" sounds while they eat, and who enjoy what you prepare for them as much as Willem.

www.customr.com

HEARTY BREAKFAST SMOOTHIE

MAKES 2 LARGE GLASSES

INGREDIENTS

2 BANANAS

JUICE OF 2 ORANGES

JUICE OF 2 LEMONS

4 TABLESPOONS OF FLAXSEED MEAL

2 TABLESPOONS CHIA SEED

12 FRESH MINT LEAVES

1 HALF-INCH PIECE OF FRESH
  GINGER

5 OUNCES FROZEN MANGO CHUNKS

PREPARATION

Puree all ingredients in a blender or with a hand blender.
Serve immediately.

WILLEM

139

LUKEWARM VEGETABLE SALAD

INGREDIENTS

1 CUP QUINOA (UNCOOKED)
2 FENNEL BULBS
2 PORTOBELLO MUSHROOMS
2 HEADS RADICCHIO
1 ZUCCHINI
3 TABLESPOONS OLIVE OIL
6 TOMATOES, QUARTERED
8 SUNDRIED TOMATOES IN OIL,
   CHOPPED
1 BUNCH FRESH CILANTRO, FINELY
   CHOPPED
½ BUNCH FRESH FLAT-LEAF PARSLEY
½ BUNCH FRESH BASIL, CHOPPED
1 RED ONION, CHOPPED
2 CUPS CRUMBLED FETA
2 TABLESPOONS PUMPKIN SEEDS
2 TABLESPOONS SUNFLOWER SEEDS
JUICE OF 1 LEMON
SALT AND PEPPER, TO TASTE

PREPARATION

Prepare the quinoa following the instructions on the package. Slice the fennel, portobello mushrooms, radicchio, and zucchini and place on a grill pan. Drizzle with the olive oil and grill until tender. Then place in a large bowl.

Add the cooked quinoa into the bowl, along with the rest of the ingredients. Season with salt and pepper to taste, and serve.

142

FAVORITE SPOT IN THE KITCHEN

Behind the stove. For Willem, cooking means relaxing.

- -

DAILY SOURCE OF JOY

The handmade countertop—because it's beautiful and easy to maintain.

- -

BEST-KEPT CULINARY SECRET

Try to experiment with grilling food. Meat, for example, tastes so different when it's grilled. The shorter the cooking time, the more tender the meat becomes. And Willem loves to experiment with grilling various vegetables at the same time: you'll get this beautiful combination of crunchy and soft.

- -

FAVORITE SURPRISING FLAVOR COMBINATION

Milk chocolate with caramel and sea salt.

- -

FAVORITE SPICES AND HERBS

Ginger and coriander.

- -

INSPIRATIONS

www.jorrevanast.com
www.royalvkb.com
www.magazin.com (in Dutch only)
www.manufactum.de (in Dutch only)

- -

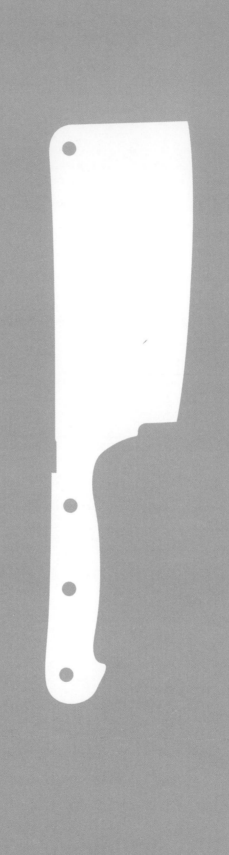

INGRID & HENK

INGRID & HENK

Ingrid and Henk share their kitchen with son Minne and daughter Pippa. The couple are the people behind *wood & wool stool*. They started making their stools from reclaimed wood with crocheted covers years ago, and they are still an international sales success.

In addition, Ingrid works part time as a sales clerk and "flower girl" at the restaurant, shop, and organic market *Villa Augustus* in Dordrecht, the Netherlands, which is also the couple's hometown.

I met Ingrid through a shared passion for *Fermob* garden furniture: together we've lugged many benches, shelves, and other pieces of furniture through various towns. And we've also taught people how to crochet.

THE KITCHEN

Ingrid and Henk chose against a standard layout for their newly-built kitchen. They didn't want a big sink unit under the windows but placed it in the corner of the kitchen instead, leaving enough space for a large dining table and a sideboard. This way there's room to dine on the left side of the kitchen and to cook on the right side. The buffet offers plenty of space for crockery and cutlery.

The entire ground floor has oak herringbone parquet. Ingrid and Henk decided against oiling the oak, so the wood would take on a beautiful weathered look over time.

The couple love timber that "lives" in general. Henk can often be found hunting for scrap wood with the couple's good friend Hans. Once Henk has brought the wood back home, he and Ingrid create beautiful objects from it, such as the backsplash behind the sink. This doesn't only look good, it also lends itself brilliantly to stacking up plates or as a display for constantly rotating flea market finds.

Besides the items found in flea markets, there are also lots of souvenirs from their travels to different countries, especially Morocco, their favorite travel destination. Almost everything in their home is impossible to buy in shops. That makes their interior personal and unique.

Henk and Ingrid love no-nonsense cooking with a tagine, preferably serving various small dishes with Turkish bread, delicious sauces, dips, and salads.

www.woodwoolstool.com

TAGINE WITH ROASTED BEETS

SERVES 6

INGREDIENTS

1 TABLESPOON OLIVE OIL
3 6-OUNCE CHICKEN BREASTS
SALT AND PEPPER, TO TASTE
2 RED BELL PEPPERS
HANDFUL OF FRESH CILANTRO,
    FINELY CHOPPED
HANDFUL OF FRESH FLAT-LEAF PARSLEY,
    FINELY CHOPPED
1 TEASPOON GROUND RAS EL HANOUT
1 TEASPOON GROUND NUTMEG
2 CLOVES OF GARLIC, CHOPPED

For the beets:
2 RED, 2 YELLOW, AND 2 WHITE BEETS
6 RED POTATOES
2 TABLESPOONS OLIVE OIL
SALT AND PEPPER, TO TASTE

For the sauce:
2 SHALLOTS
HANDFUL OF FRESH FLAT-LEAF PARSLEY
HANDFUL OF FRESH CILANTRO
2 TABLESPOONS SPICY MUSTARD
1 TABLESPOON WHITE WINE VINEGAR
1 TABLESPOON OLIVE OIL
½ CUP COLD WATER

PREPARATION

Pour olive oil in the tagine dish. Sprinkle the chicken with salt and pepper to taste, and place them in the tagine. Place the (whole) bell peppers on top of them. In a small bowl, mix the cilantro, parsley, spices, and garlic and then sprinkle over the chicken and the bell peppers. Cover with lid and cook over low heat for 3 hours. If you're using a gas range, use a heat diffuser.

For the beets:
Preheat the oven to 400°F. Cut all the beets in quarters and the potatoes into thick slices. Place the beets and potatoes in a large baking dish. Pour the olive oil over the vegetables and season with plenty of salt and pepper. Place in the oven for 20 minutes (shake the dish or give the vegetables a quick stir every once in a while to prevent them from sticking to the bottom of the dish).

For the sauce:
Finely chop the shallots, parsley, and cilantro. Mix with the rest of the sauce ingredients.

Pour the sauce over the chicken and beets and serve.

PUMPKIN CHICKPEA SALAD

SERVES 6

INGREDIENTS

1 PUMPKIN (ABOUT 14 OUNCES)
4 TABLESPOONS OLIVE OIL, DIVIDED
1 TEASPOON GROUND CORIANDER
1 TEASPOON GROUND CUMIN
1 TABLESPOON SALT
1 TABLESPOON PEPPER
4 RIPE FIGS
HANDFUL OF FRESH CILANTRO
1 RED ONION
1 15-OUNCE CAN CHICKPEAS
   (DRAINED AND PATTED DRY)
JUICE AND ZEST OF 1 LEMON

PREPARATION

Preheat the oven to 400°F. Peel and cut the pumpkin into bite-sized chunks. In a bowl, mix the pumpkin chunks, 2 tablespoons of the olive oil, coriander, cumin, salt, and pepper. Place the mixture in a medium-sized baking dish and roast for 20 minutes.

In the meantime, chop the figs and cilantro, slice the onion, and place in a large bowl. Mix in the roasted pumpkin and chickpeas. Add the remaining 2 tablespoons olive oil, the lemon zest, and lemon juice. Mix well and serve.

BAKLAVA

MAKES ABOUT 8 PIECES

INGREDIENTS

1 CUP SHELLED PISTACHIOS

1¾ CUPS WALNUTS

2 TABLESPOONS LIGHT BROWN
   SUGAR

1 TEASPOON GROUND CINNAMON

½ CUP UNSALTED BUTTER

10 SHEETS READY-TO-USE PHYLLO
   DOUGH

For the syrup:

1 CUP SUPERFINE SUGAR

¾ CUP COLD WATER

½ CUP HONEY

1 TEASPOON VANILLA EXTRACT

PREPARATION

Preheat the oven to 350°F. Grease an 8" x 8" baking pan, using a generous amount of butter. Mince the pistachios and walnuts with a food processor or blender. Place the nuts into a medium bowl and mix in the sugar and cinnamon, and set aside.

In a small saucepan, over low heat, melt the butter, and then remove from heat. Place the first sheet of phyllo dough into the baking pan. Brush the top of the phyllo with a layer of melted butter. Repeat this step for the next four sheets, buttering the top of the last sheet as well.

Spread the nut mixture over the fifth layer of phyllo. Place the next five layers of phyllo on top of the nuts, again buttering in between each layer of phyllo. Using a sharp knife, cut diamond or square shapes into the top layer of the phyllo. Bake for 20 minutes. Take out of the oven and carefully cut into pieces following the pre-cut lines.

For the syrup:

Warm up all ingredients in a small saucepan over low heat for about 20 minutes, until you get a syrupy mixture. Place the baking pan with the baklava on a large plate, and pour the hot syrup over the warm baklava (sometimes the syrup may drip over the edges of the pan). Serve when the syrup has been properly absorbed.

FAVORITE SPOT IN THE KITCHEN

The dining table, and the countertop with the sink in the corner of the room.

~~~~~~~~~~~~~~~~~~~~~~~~~~~~~~

DAILY SOURCE OF JOY

The backsplash made out of scrap wood, which has been there for the past ten years, is still a success. They're also happy with the efficient layout of the kitchen, the cupboard, and the vintage service trolley.

~~~~~~~~~~~~~~~~~~~~~~~~~~~~~~

BEST-KEPT KITCHEN SECRET

Everything will sparkle if you scrub it with old-fashioned green household soap.

~~~~~~~~~~~~~~~~~~~~~~~~~~~~~~

FAVORITE SURPRISING FLAVOR COMBINATION

Fresh figs, avocado, and mango.

~~~~~~~~~~~~~~~~~~~~~~~~~~~~~~

FAVORITE SPICES AND HERBS

Tagine spices, garlic, and fresh coriander.

~~~~~~~~~~~~~~~~~~~~~~~~~~~~~~

INSPIRATIONS

www.villa-augustus.nl
www.anthropologie.com

~~~~~~~~~~~~~~~~~~~~~~~~~~~~~~

ANNEMIE & JAN

ANNEMIE & JAN

A hidden dirt road, which branches off a main road in the Belgian village of Herenthout, leads to the country estate of my friend Ellen's former in-laws Annemie and Jan. They share it with their cat Zappa, Roger the rooster, the chicken Madeleine, and four donkeys. One of the donkeys is called George, because he was born on the same day as Prince George of Cambridge.

THE KITCHEN

Annemie and Jan's kitchen is open to the garden on one side. They eat in this semi-outdoor kitchen in all weather—even when it snows. The large fireplace and the pizza oven keep everyone warm. Friends and family know to dress warmly when they come to visit the couple in winter, as they know they'll be eating outside. In addition, the hostess always has extra blankets for warmth and coziness handy. In hot summers, the canopy provides shade and coolness.

Annemie and Jan built the entire kitchen from scratch, often using materials and objects they found in abandoned buildings or faraway places. The stone sink in the kitchen comes from a Belgian bar that had closed down; the faucet was bought on a trip to Venice.

The large window overlooks a cornfield and is like having an ever-changing painting on the wall. As the seasons pass by, the view is never once the same. Sometimes a pheasant will run past, or a hare jumps out of the shrubbery.

The couple are great hosts. They often dine until deep in the night with their guests. If someone feels like gazing into the cosmos, they can use the telescope and look for shooting stars and comets.

Annemie and Jan pick fresh herbs from their herb garden and in September they harvest the grapes from the vines that are overgrowing the canopy. There is a swimming pool, too, for cooling down after a busy day of gardening on hot summer days or just to relax by. Annemie and Jan really have created their own paradise on earth.

CHEESE DIP POT

SERVES 1

INGREDIENTS
½ CUP CRUMBLED FETA
OLIVE OIL
1 CLOVE OF GARLIC
1 SPRIG FRESH OREGANO
1 TOMATO
SALT AND PEPPER, TO TASTE

PREPARATION
Preheat the oven to 300°F. Cover the bottom of an 8-ounce ramekin with the feta. Pour olive oil over the feta, until the feta is just submerged. Slice the garlic into thin slices and layer them over the feta. Pluck the oregano leaves off the sprig and place on top of the garlic. Remove the seeds from the tomato and cut the tomato into small pieces. Place on top of the oregano and season with salt and pepper. Place the covered pot in the oven for 20 minutes.

Serve with bread.

GINGER
CHEESECAKE

MAKES 1 9-INCH CAKE

INGREDIENTS

For the base:

2 TABLESPOONS UNSALTED BUTTER

7 OUNCES GINGER SNAPS

For the batter:

2 CUPS RICOTTA

½ CUP CREAM CHEESE

3 EGG YOLKS

⅔ CUP SUPERFINE SUGAR

1 TEASPOON VANILLA EXTRACT

1 TABLESPOON GINGER SYRUP

1 TABLESPOON STEM GINGER IN SYRUP

1 TABLESPOON ALL-PURPOSE WHEAT FLOUR

For the garnish:

FRESH RASPBERRIES

PREPARATION

Preheat the oven to 350°F. Grease a 9-inch spring form pan with butter and line with parchment paper, making sure the paper goes all the way to the edges.

Melt the butter in a small saucepan over low heat. Crumble the ginger snaps in a food processor. In a medium bowl, mix the cookie crumbs with the melted butter. Using the underside of a spoon, press the mixture evenly across the bottom of the spring form. Put in the fridge until the batter is ready.

Mix the ricotta and the cream cheese in a blender or food processor. Add the other ingredients one by one, mixing until combined. Scoop the mixture over the cake base and bake for 25 to 30 minutes. The cake is ready when the batter doesn't move when you gently shake the form.

Let cool completely, and then sprinkle the raspberries on top.

FAVORITE SPOT IN THE KITCHEN

The large table in the semi-outdoor kitchen. It's a great place for preparing food or to have an aperitif. You feel connected to the outdoors, being by the garden with the rooster and chicken. In summer, you're close to the sunshine but protected from the heat by the canopy.

◇◇◇◇◇◇◇◇◇◇◇◇◇◇◇◇◇◇◇◇◇◇◇◇◇◇◇◇

DAILY SOURCE OF JOY

That table. And the pizza oven, for all the *oohs* and *aahs* it gets from admiring guests.

◇◇◇◇◇◇◇◇◇◇◇◇◇◇◇◇◇◇◇◇◇◇◇◇◇◇◇◇

BEST-KEPT CULINARY SECRET

Prepare as much as possible the night before a party, leaving plenty of time on the day to lay the table and put up decorations. They love to give themed dinner parties matching the music and the decorations to the theme they've planned. They also keep track of all the dishes they've made and who they've served them to. That way their guests will never be served something twice.

◇◇◇◇◇◇◇◇◇◇◇◇◇◇◇◇◇◇◇◇◇◇◇◇◇◇◇◇

FAVORITE SURPRISING FLAVOR COMBINATION

Pink peppercorns in a yogurt-and-chives sauce.

◇◇◇◇◇◇◇◇◇◇◇◇◇◇◇◇◇◇◇◇◇◇◇◇◇◇◇◇

FAVORITE SPICES AND HERBS

Nutmeg and fresh rosemary.

◇◇◇◇◇◇◇◇◇◇◇◇◇◇◇◇◇◇◇◇◇◇◇◇◇◇◇◇

INSPIRATIONS

www.lecreuset.com

◇◇◇◇◇◇◇◇◇◇◇◇◇◇◇◇◇◇◇◇◇◇◇◇◇◇◇◇

DAAN & JAN

DAAN & JAN

Daan is a mother, creative entrepreneur, blogger, and the wife of artist, musician, translator, and writer Jan Rot. They live in an old mansion in the south of the Netherlands; a stone's throw away from Joscha and Erwin *(see page 113)* and the port of the Belgian city Antwerp.

They share their kitchen with their daughters Elvis and Maantje Piet and their sons Rover and Wolf.

Daan is a blogger and girl-trip friend of mine *(see page 114)*.

THE KITCHEN

Daan, Jan, and their children live in their own version of Pippi Longstocking's *Villa Villekulla—Villa* stands for "mansion" and *Villekulla* for "many colors." Not only is Daan and Jan's mansion painted in many colors, but also, the family themselves are anything but bland. When you enter the magnificent hall with its marble floors, ornamented ceiling, and high walls, you stumble over mountains of boxes and dozens of coats, shoes, and bags. But it's such a beautiful mess: everything goes together. That is the art of Daan and Jan.

Family friend and designer Simon de Boer helped them with some interior rearrangements. What used to be two reception rooms divided by sliding doors is now an informal front room and a kitchen; in between them is a floating wall with a bookcase on one side and kitchen cabinets on the other.

The kitchen cabinets are made partly from stainless steel and partly from MDF, painted in green. Daan has filled the shelves with all sorts of decorative kitchen stuff. Nice jars, pretty tea boxes, tins with pictures of the Dutch king Willem-Alexander and his queen Máxima, and teapots that Daan has designed herself. In Daan and Jan's kitchen, beautiful things are allowed to be on display. The walls are covered in drawings by the couple's children and posters advertising Jan's past performances, kept in the kitchen as mementos.

The family doesn't eat red meat but they do like chicken and fish. And they love sushi. The table is always laid like a medieval banquet, offering plenty of choices in all kinds of deliciousness. Their kitchen cart by *IKEA* is used for storing fruit and vegetables, and it's always overflowing, because Daan would rather have too much in the house than too little.

www.maandagdaandag.blogspot.com (in Dutch only)
www.janrot.nl (in Dutch only)

BOEKOE KITA

MIJN LITTLE ITALY

hummingbird cookbook

ciao bella

PLENTY

Het derde NRC HANDELSBLAD kookboek

Koninklijke gerechten voor keuken-prinsen & prinsessen

Het koeken

Brunch!

Toon Tellegen
Taartenboek
Met recepten van
Henja Schneider
QUERIDO

De

Taarten van Abel

R O T J E S

DAAN & JAN

GUACAMOLE

MAKES 1 BOWL

INGREDIENTS
2 RIPE AVOCADOS, PEELED
2 TOMATOES
1 RED ONION
1 CLOVE OF GARLIC
SALT AND PEPPER, TO TASTE

PREPARATION
In a large bowl, mash the avocados with a fork. Chop the tomatoes, onion, and garlic and add them to the bowl. Season with salt and pepper to taste, and serve with nacho chips and sour cream.

Tip
To make it a little spicy, add a minced red chili pepper to the guacamole.

DAAN & JAN

SUSHI WITH ROASTED ASPARAGUS TIPS

MAKES 2 ROLLS WITH 6 TO 8 PIECES OF SUSHI EACH

INGREDIENTS

1½ CUPS (ABOUT 8.8 OUNCES)
  SUSHI RICE
1 CUP WATER
1 TABLESPOON MIRIN (RICE WINE)
20 ASPARAGUS TIPS
OLIVE OIL
COARSE SEA SALT AND PEPPER,
  TO TASTE
2 NORI SHEETS
3 OUNCES NORWEGIAN SMOKED
  SALMON SLICES
VARIOUS TYPES OF LEEK SHOOTS
  AND OTHER SPROUTS
1 TABLESPOON MAYONNAISE

PREPARATION

Preheat the oven to 350°F. Place the sushi rice in a medium pot and add the water. Place over high heat and bring to a boil, stirring occasionally. Once it comes up to a boil, turn down the heat to low, cover and continue to cook for about 5 to 7 minutes or until it's soft and sticky. Let it cool down, mix in the mirin, and set aside.

Place the asparagus tips in a baking dish and drizzle with olive oil and sea salt. Roast for 15 minutes. Remove and set aside.

Place a nori sheet on a sushi mat. Heap a spoonful of sushi rice in the middle of the sheet and press it out evenly over the sheet—but not all the way to the edges, and leave about 1½ inches at the bottom uncovered. (You may need to dip your fingers in water, as the rice will be very sticky to work with.) Next take a few of the asparagus tips and lay them horizontally in the center of the rice. Repeat with the salmon, and then add some leek shoots, or other sprouts, on top. Add a dash of mayonnaise and season with salt and pepper to taste. Carefully roll up the mat, squeezing tightly. (The video on my website will help you visualize how to do this!) Then remove the roll from the mat and cut into slices.

CHOCOLATE CHEESECAKE JARS

MAKES 6 LARGE, OR 12 SMALL, JARS

INGREDIENTS
7 OUNCES DARK CHOCOLATE
1 CUP PRESSED COTTAGE CHEESE*
1½ CUPS CREAM CHEESE
3 TABLESPOONS SUPERFINE SUGAR
1 TEASPOON VANILLA EXTRACT
¾ CUP + 1 TABLESPOON HEAVY
   CREAM
16 OREO COOKIES
6 OR 12 SPRIGS FRESH MINT

PREPARATION
Melt the chocolate in a small saucepan over low heat, stirring constantly. Then remove from heat. In a large bowl, beat the pressed cottage cheese, cream cheese, sugar, and vanilla. Then mix in the melted chocolate. Next, slowly add the heavy cream while continuing to beat for about two minutes, until well-blended.

Distribute evenly into the jars. Place in fridge for two hours or until firm.

Twist the sides of the Oreo cookies apart, scrape out the filling with a knife. Crumble just the cookies (without the filling), and sprinkle evenly among the jars. Decorate each jar with a fresh mint twig.

If you can't find pressed cottage cheese, you can make your own by draining 1¼ cup regular cottage cheese in a fine sieve to remove the liquid.

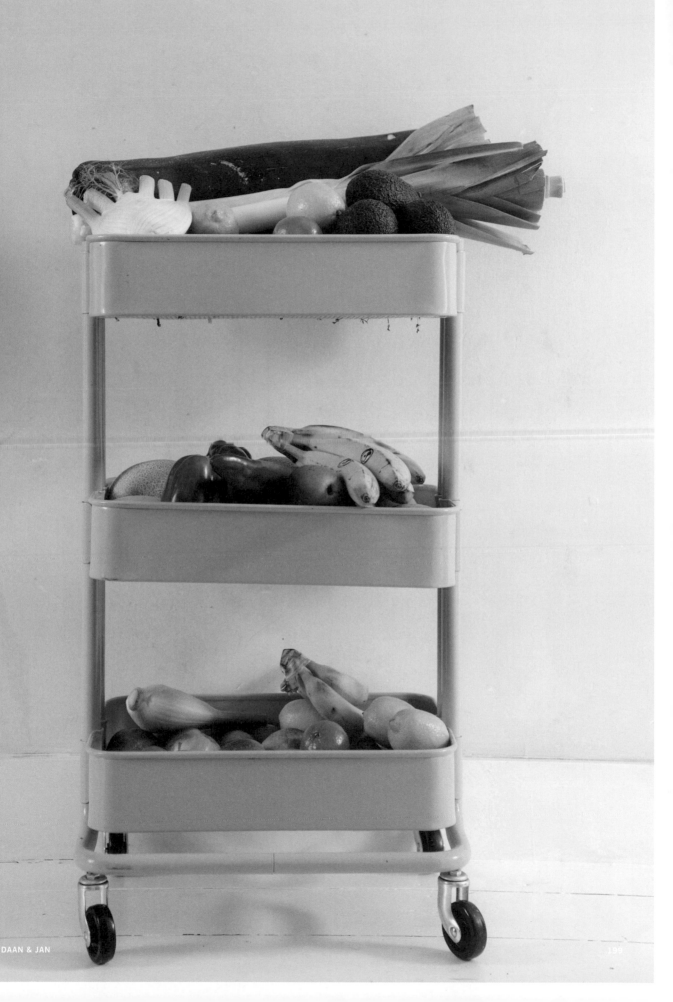

FAVORITE SPOT IN THE KITCHEN

The dining table, where the family meets: one does their homework and the other reads the newspaper, while a pot of soup is bubbling on the stove and a crackling fire is lit in the front room fireplace.

~~~~~~~~~~~~~~~~~~~~~~~~~~~~~~~~

DAILY SOURCE OF JOY

The bookshelf with the cookbooks facing forward gets Daan into a cooking frenzy. And the counter with a view of the dining table—a setup that makes cooking, especially preparing pancakes, particularly fun. There's nothing as satisfying as being encouraged by a table full of hungry children.

~~~~~~~~~~~~~~~~~~~~~~~~~~~~~~~~

BEST-KEPT CULINARY SECRET

Butter makes everything taste better.

~~~~~~~~~~~~~~~~~~~~~~~~~~~~~~~~

FAVORITE SURPRISING FLAVOR COMBINATION

Brown beans with onions and peppers, topped with a thick layer of apple syrup.

~~~~~~~~~~~~~~~~~~~~~~~~~~~~~~~~

FAVORITE SPICES AND HERBS

Cinnamon and fresh mint.

~~~~~~~~~~~~~~~~~~~~~~~~~~~~~~~~

INSPIRATIONS

www.madame-charlotte.nl (in Dutch only)
www.mmezsazsaordent.blogspot.com (in Dutch only)
www.deyummyblogsisters.com (in Dutch only)

~~~~~~~~~~~~~~~~~~~~~~~~~~~~~~~~

ANNE-MARIE & HARRY

ANNE-MARIE & HARRY

Restaurant *Villa Bloemenhof* is located in a small village in the south of the Netherlands. In addition to being a restaurant, it is also the home of my sister Anne-Marie and her husband Harry.

In their living room-style restaurant, Anne-Marie is the hostess and Harry the chef. From Wednesdays through Sundays, they share the kitchen with chef Frank and waiter Ron. Together, they serve the most delicious food to their—on average—45 customers a day.

THE KITCHEN

The front room, upstairs, and attic of the stately old mansion that is *Villa Bloemenhof* serve as living quarters for Anne-Marie and Harry. The rest of the ground floor houses the restaurant. Anne-Marie and Harry didn't change much to the original layout of the house when they bought it 17 years ago. However, the former garage has become the restaurant's kitchen, and where the old kitchen used to be are now the restaurant's guest bathrooms and the cloakroom. The restaurant itself takes up a suite of rooms and a conservatory. Thanks to the homely atmosphere and the warm welcome, it feels like you're more than just dining at Anne-Marie and Harry's restaurant: you're also visiting them.

Anne-Marie and I were raised by creative parents. No wonder we both love decorating. You can see this in the interior of the restaurant: Anne-Marie has chosen cool, yet elegant leather chairs by the Italian brand *Poltrona Frau*, leather rugs by *Pachamama*, a chandelier by the Belgian brand *Brand van Egmond* and beautiful wooden tables by *Pols Potten*.

Anne-Marie and Harry use the front room of the ground floor as their downstairs living room. Anne-Marie does her administration in this room and Harry uses it to browse books and magazines in search for inspiration for new recipes. An hour before the restaurant opens, they have dinner with Frank and Ron here. The large, unusual lamp shade above the table is from *DK Home* and lends a kind of surreal tension to the room.

You can find African art throughout my sister's home and restaurant. Anne-Marie has a strong affinity for South Africa, maybe because that's where our roots are: we are the daughters of an Afro-Surinamese, a Surinamese Creole.

On Mondays and Tuesdays, when the restaurant is closed, my sister and her husband like to eat out at other restaurants or soak up some sun on the Spanish island of Majorca, where they often travel for new ideas and recipes for their restaurant.

www.villabloemenhof.com (in Dutch only)
shop.villabloemenhof.com

ANNE-MARIE

SALMON TART

MAKES 1 TART

INGREDIENTS
2 MEDIUM-SIZED WAXY POTATOES
1.75 TO 2 OUNCES SALMON
SALT AND PEPPER, TO TASTE
1 TEASPOON OLIVE OIL
1 PLUM TOMATO
2 OUNCES MOZZARELLA
BUNCH OF FRESH BASIL

For the dressing:
JUICE OF ½ LEMON
2 TABLESPOONS MAYONNAISE

PREPARATION
Place the potatoes in a small pot and cover with about 1 inch of cold water. Over medium to high heat, bring the water to a boil. Then reduce the heat to a simmer and cook the potatoes until they can be easily pierced with a fork. Drain the potatoes and set aside.

Season the salmon with salt and pepper to taste. Heat the olive oil in a frying pan and add the salmon. Fry on both sides until the salmon is soft (about 5 minutes). Remove from pan and set aside.

Cut the tomato, mozzarella, potatoes, and salmon into small pieces. Coarsely chop the basil. Make the dressing by whisking the lemon juice with the mayonnaise in a small bowl.

Grease a ring mold (3" diameter x 5.5" high) with olive oil and place on a plate. Fill it as follows:
1. potatoes
2. basil
3. dash of olive oil
4. tomatoes
5. salmon
6. dressing
7. mozzarella

Then carefully lift the mold and garnish with a basil leaf.

Tip:
You can make a ring mold yourself by cutting a piece of plastic pipe to size.

ANNE-MARIE & HARRY

TROPICAL PAVLOVA

INGREDIENTS

6 PASSION FRUIT

1 TABLESPOON ALIZÉ GOLD
  PASSION LIQUEUR

1 TEASPOON FRUIT PECTIN

1 MANGO (ABOUT 7 OUNCES)

7 OUNCES PINEAPPLE

7 OUNCES VANILLA MERINGUES

1 CAN OF WHIPPED CREAM

HANDFUL OF PISTACHIOS, CHOPPED

PREPARATION

Cut the passion fruit in half and, using a spoon, scrape the pulp into a small pot. Add the liqueur and the fruit pectin and cook on low heat until the mixture has turned into a slushy sauce.

Cut the mango and the pineapple into bite-sized chunks and distribute evenly among four dessert bowls. Pour the sauce over the fruit—about one tablespoon per bowl.

Crumble the meringues over the fruit and sauce. Spray some whipped cream on top and garnish with the pistachios.

214

FAVORITE SPOT IN THE HOUSE

The front room, because it also functions as the dining room and living room.

DAILY SOURCE OF JOY

The coffee maker by the designer *Kees van der Westen*, because of its beautiful design.

BEST-KEPT CULINARY SECRET

Using ginger as a substitute for sugar. There are a lot of beautiful and surprising things you can do with ginger.

FAVORITE SURPRISING FLAVOR COMBINATION

White chocolate and garlic.

FAVORITE SPICES AND HERBS

Ras el hanout and the Javanese Djawa curry spice mix.

INSPIRATIONS

www.keesvanderwesten.com
www.polspotten.nl
www.brostecopenhagen.com
www.serax.com
www.basketsbeadsbasics.nl

CLAUDETTE & PAUL

CLAUDETTE & PAUL

What was once a boys' school just outside the city center of Utrecht in the Netherlands is now the home of Claudette and Paul. Together with their son Faas, their daughter Jet, and Clara, an Argentinian exchange student who's the family's guest for a year, they live in two former classrooms, the old boiler room, and a part of the attic. Claudette runs *Snor Publishing*, the original publisher of this book (first published in Dutch), with Anne-marieke *(see page 237)*.

THE KITCHEN

Through the backyard (formerly the school playground) you step inside Claudette and Paul's kitchen. Some things are immediately striking: the big lamp shade above the dining table, the height of the ceilings and the various different levels of the room. For example, there is a plateau above the cooking area containing a hangout space for kids. You can look down from it onto the dining table, which was made by Paul's father.

Jos Otten, an uncle of Claudette's, designed and built the kitchen. With the help of Annelies at the concept store *Strand West* in Utrecht, Claudette and Paul created a color palette and picked out wallpaper and curtains. Featuring high-quality equipment and simple but smart solutions, the kitchen is every amateur chef's dream.

The kitchen island is on wheels and thus easy to move around. If the couple need extra space for a party they just wheel the island out of the kitchen. Uncle Jos also built the matching cupboard and shelves where Claudette stores her beautiful china. The wallpaper behind the cupboard and shelves is by *Eijffinger* and runs all the way up to the ceiling, giving the otherwise sleek kitchen a touch of frivolity.

Weekends are for big family breakfasts at the large dining table. The family buys fresh bread from *Bond & Smolders*, the best bakery in Utrecht, and cheese from a local cheese shop. When friends come over for dinner the table is the heart of the home. Claudette will hunt for delicious recipes and buy ingredients from the local farmers' market or the local independent shops.

Claudette and Paul often eat salad with their dinner and also try to feed their children at least about a half-pound of vegetables every day. Meat is not served on a daily basis, although a hearty beef stew or an oven-roasted chicken are quite the family favorites.

www.uitgeverijsnor.nl

MANGO SALAD

INGREDIENTS

1½ CUPS BEAN SPROUTS
1 BAG (ABOUT 4 OUNCES) OF
   MIXED LETTUCE
1 RED BELL PEPPER
1 RIPE AVOCADO
1 RIPE MANGO
HANDFUL OF SALTED CASHEWS
HANDFUL OF FRESH CILANTRO
HANDFUL OF FRESH MINT
½ BUNCH FLAT-LEAF PARSLEY

For the dressing:
JUICE OF 1 LIME
2 TABLESPOONS SUNFLOWER OIL
1 TEASPOON LIGHT BROWN SUGAR
1 TEASPOON RED CURRY PASTE
1 RED CHILI PEPPER
SALT AND PEPPER, TO TASTE

PREPARATION

Place the bean sprouts in a colander and pour boiling water over them. Rinse with cold water, remove excess water, and set aside. Place the lettuce in a large bowl. Cut the bell pepper, avocado, and mango into bite-sized chunks and mix in with the lettuce, adding the bean sprouts in the process. Roughly chop the cashews and finely chop the herbs and sprinkle over the salad.

In a small bowl, mix the dressing ingredients, seasoning with salt and pepper to taste. Add the dressing to the salad bowl and mix. Serve.

SALMON WITH SPICY SWEET AND SOUR SAUCE

SERVES 4

INGREDIENTS
1½ POUNDS SALMON FILLET
1 CLOVE OF GARLIC
½ CUP DARK SWEET SOY SAUCE
2 TEASPOONS BALSAMIC VINEGAR
1 TABLESPOON DARK BROWN SUGAR
1 TEASPOON SAMBAL*
8 SPRIGS OF THYME

PREPARATION
Preheat the oven to 400°F. Place the salmon in a medium-sized baking dish. Crush the garlic and add to a small bowl. Mix in the remaining ingredients, except for the thyme. Pour this mixture over the salmon. Let marinate for a half hour at room temperature and then bake for 15 minutes. Garnish with thyme sprigs.

Sambal is a spicy condiment sauce that can be found in Indian or Southeast Asian markets.

CLAUDETTE & PAUL

BEEF STEW

INGREDIENTS

- 2 POUNDS BEEF STEW MEAT
- 3 CLOVES OF GARLIC, CHOPPED
- 1 WHITE ONION, CHOPPED
- ½ POUND WHOLE CHESTNUT (OR CRIMINI) MUSHROOMS
- 3 DRIED BAY LEAVES
- 2 BEEF BOUILLON CUBES
- ¾ BOTTLE OF RED WINE
- SALT AND PEPPER, TO TASTE
- 3 SLICES GINGERBREAD CAKE*

PREPARATION

Preheat the oven to 350°F. Cut the beef into about 1-inch cubes and place them in a Dutch oven. Add the garlic, onion, mushrooms, and bay leaves to the beef. Crumble the bouillon cubes over the beef and pour the red wine in. (The beef should be just submerged—add some water if necessary.) Season with a pinch of salt and pepper, and cover. Cook in the oven for about 3 hours, until the meat is tender.

Thicken the sauce by crumbling the gingerbread cake into it. The cake should dissolve completely.

Serve with fries, rice, or mashed potatoes.

Gingerbread cake in beef stew? Yes! It may sound unusual, but give it a try. In the Netherlands, gingerbread cakes are commonly found premade in stores. If you can't buy one, you may have to make your own—but it's worth it!

FAVORITE SPOT IN THE KITCHEN

The chopping block on the kitchen island, where people hang out, chat, and read cookbooks, but which is also great for everything from chopping herbs to rolling out dough. It has enough space for several people working simultaneously, too. The family has drawn up a cooking schedule: the children each do the grocery shopping, cooking, and cleaning up once a week.

~~~~~~~~~~~~~~~~

DAILY SOURCE OF JOY

The well-thought-out details of Claudette's uncle's kitchen design. The counters are completely custom made, and have exactly the right height (goodbye back pains from cooking) and depth (lots of extra space). Claudette also loves the large dining table in the kitchen.

~~~~~~~~~~~~~~~~

BEST-KEPT KITCHEN SECRET

The dishwasher is positioned slightly higher than normal, about 15 inches from the ground. This way you don't have to bend down so much when loading it, and nobody ever trips over an open dishwasher door.

~~~~~~~~~~~~~~~~

FAVORITE SURPRISING FLAVOR COMBINATION

Cayenne pepper with sugar, pomegranate syrup, and maple syrup: a combination inspired by Yotam Ottolenghi, the London-based chef and cookbook writer much beloved by Claudette.

~~~~~~~~~~~~~~~~

FAVORITE SPICES AND HERBS

Handfuls of fresh cilantro, flat-leaf parsley, and fresh mint.

~~~~~~~~~~~~~~~~

INSPIRATIONS

www.kinfolk.com
www.readcereal.com
www.planetatangerina.com/en
www.fleurmonde.com

~~~~~~~~~~~~~~~~

ANNEMARIEKE & GERARD

ANNEMARIEKE & GERARD

Annemarieke, co-owner of *Snor Publishing*, and Gerard share their kitchen with sons Bram and Wickie, daughter Pleuntje, and two very old cats. Their open-plan kitchen (and the rest of the house) is located in a former public elementary school in a vibrant neighborhood called Lombok, in the Dutch city of Utrecht.

THE KITCHEN

The former school building where Annemarieke and Gerard live with their children is completely different from the former school building in which publishing companion Claudette *(see page 219)* lives. The large open spaces and high ceilings are reminiscent of a loft and most of their living area is on one floor. Various mezzanines create additional levels and serve as room dividers.

As it often happens during renovations, Annemarieke and Gerard ran out of money when they decorated their home and there was not enough left for the *Vipp* kitchen units they had envisioned. As an alternative, they chose secondhand *IKEA* cabinets with new doors and worktops by *Internorm*. To pick up the secondhand refrigerator they drove to another city in a van. That's the power of secondhand marketplaces on the Internet: not only do you recycle items, but you also get to take a trip, meet the people who sell the respective items, and take a peek inside their homes.

Annemarieke instantly fell in love with the large blackbird poster by *Maartje van den Noort* when she first saw it at a trade show in Amsterdam. The poster is now the main eye-catcher in the kitchen. The black *Tom Dixon* lights above the sturdy, rugged wooden dining table are a beautiful match. Because of the open-plan layout, the living room area's stacked *IKEA* Expedit bookshelves give a color boost to the kitchen, too. Plenty of fresh flowers and potted plants make the room even more colorful and homey.

The combination of old and new, of used furniture, designer furniture, and *IKEA*, is very refreshing, bold, and eclectic—yet the overall impression is harmonious.

The family likes to do their shopping in the nearby *Kanaalstraat* in Lombok. It's a street that's known for its many stores offering a large range of exotic foods and spices. Nowhere else in Utrecht can you find Turkish, Moroccan, Chinese, and Surinamese stores together on one street. They go there on Saturdays to buy delicious tapenade, Turkish bread, and eggplant rolls—the *Kanaalstraat* in Utrecht really is one big food fest.

www.uitgeverijsnor.nl

CHICKEN SAAG WITH NAAN

SERVES 4

INGREDIENTS
1 POUND SPINACH (ABOUT 4 CUPS)
1 RED CHILI PEPPER
½-INCH PIECE FRESH GINGER
HANDFUL FRESH CILANTRO
2 CLOVES OF GARLIC
1 RED ONION
JUICE OF 1 LEMON
1 POUND OF BONELESS CHICKEN
   BREASTS
2 TABLESPOONS OLIVE OIL
SALT AND PEPPER, TO TASTE
1¾ CUPS COCONUT MILK
2 TABLESPOONS KORMA CURRY
   PASTE

For the naan:
½ CUP REDUCED-FAT MILK
½ CUP LOW-FAT YOGURT
¼ CUP BOILING WATER
1 TEASPOON INSTANT DRY YEAST
½ TEASPOON BAKING SODA
1 TEASPOON SUPERFINE SUGAR
¾ TEASPOON SALT
2¾ CUPS ALL-PURPOSE WHEAT
   FLOUR
4 CLOVES OF GARLIC
4 TABLESPOONS OLIVE OIL

PREPARATION
Mince the spinach, red chili pepper, ginger, cilantro, garlic, and onion in a food processor. Add the lemon juice and mix. Cut the chicken into large chunks. Heat the oil in a large frying pan over medium heat and add the chicken. Season with salt and pepper to taste and cook until the chicken is golden brown and cooked through. Add the minced ingredients to the pan, and stir. Then add the coconut milk and curry paste. Stir well and simmer over low heat until creamy.

For the naan:
In a large bowl, mix the milk, yogurt, and boiling water with a wooden spoon until smooth. Add the yeast, baking soda, sugar, salt, and flour. Mix until you have a soft, sticky dough. Cover the bowl with a moist dish cloth and set aside for 30 minutes. Dust some flour over the dough, knead briefly, cover again, and set aside for an hour.

Dust your worktop with plenty of flour and form the dough into a ball. Cut the dough into quarters. Roll out the pieces into oval shapes that are about ½ to 1 inch thick. Keep dusting both sides with flour in the process. Set aside.

Crush the garlic and mix with the olive oil in a small bowl. Heat a frying pan and warm up the olive oil with the garlic over low to medium heat. Brush the dough pieces with the garlic oil and add to the frying pan. Cook on both sides until lightly brown.

ANNEMARIEKE & GERARD

BRAM'S LASAGNA

SERVES 4

INGREDIENTS

4 SMALL CARROTS

1 WHITE ONION

2 TABLESPOONS OLIVE OIL

2 CLOVES OF GARLIC, CRUSHED

12 OUNCES MINCED BEEF

24-OUNCE JAR TOMATO-AND-BASIL
   PASTA SAUCE

1 CUP WATER

SALT AND PEPPER, TO TASTE

1 TABLESPOON DRIED BASIL

16-OUNCE BOX LASAGNA

15-OUNCE JAR BÉCHAMEL

1¾ CUPS GRATED PARMESAN
   CHEESE

PREPARATION

Preheat the oven to 400°F. Slice the carrots and chop the onion. Heat the oil in a large frying pan over medium to high heat and add the carrots and onion. Cook for about 2 to 3 minutes. Add the garlic and stir. While continuing to stir, add in the minced meat. Then add the pasta sauce, water, salt and pepper to taste, and the basil and let simmer for 30 minutes.

Prepare the lasagna per the instructions on the box.

In a 9" x 13" dish layer the ingredients in the following order:
   Layer 1: beef
   Layer 2: béchamel
   Layer 3: lasagna
   Layer 4: beef
   Layer 5: béchamel
   Layer 6: lasagna
   Layer 7: beef
   Layer 8: parmesan cheese

Cook, uncovered, in the oven for 30 minutes.

RASPBERRY AND MADEIRA CAKE TRIFLE

SERVES 4

INGREDIENTS

¾ CUP UNSALTED BUTTER, ROOM
    TEMPERATURE
¾ CUP + 2 TABLESPOONS LIGHT
    BROWN SUGAR
ZEST OF 1 LEMON
1 TEASPOON VANILLA EXTRACT
3 EGGS
1½ CUPS + 1 TABLESPOON
    SELF-RISING FLOUR
½ CUP CHOPPED ALMONDS
DASH OF MILK

For the trifle:
1 CUP (ABOUT 8.8 OUNCES)
    MASCARPONE
½ CUP CRÈME FRAÎCHE
1 TO 1¼ CUPS FRESH RASPBERRIES,
    DIVIDED
1 TABLESPOON LIGHT BROWN SUGAR

PREPARATION

Preheat the oven to 325°F. In a medium bowl, beat the butter and sugar together until smooth. Add the lemon zest and the vanilla extract. Then beat the eggs in one at a time. Slowly add the flour and almonds and combine. Stir in a dash of milk.

Pour the batter into a greased 7-inch loaf pan and bake for 50 minutes. Let cool down completely and turn out the cake onto a chopping board. Cut the cake to fit the glasses that you want to serve the trifle in.

For the trifle:
In a medium bowl, mix the mascarpone and the crème fraîche until you have a thick cream. In a food processor puree half of the raspberries and then mix with the sugar in a small bowl.

Fill the trifle glasses in the following order:
    Layer 1: cake
    Layer 2: cream
    Layer 3: raspberry puree
    Layer 4: cake
    Layer 5: cream
    Layer 6: whole raspberries

Fun fact: The name Madeira cake has its roots in an 18th-century English custom to serve a slice of the cake with a glass of Madeira wine.

FAVORITE SPOT IN THE KITCHEN

Annemarieke really likes to drink a glass of wine at one end of the kitchen island while Gerard cooks up something really delicious at the other end.

◇◇◇◇◇◇◇◇◇◇◇◇◇◇◇◇◇◇◇◇◇◇◇◇◇◇◇◇◇◇◇◇◇◇◇◇◇

DAILY SOURCE OF JOY

All the space! Additionally, the fact that the refrigerator and oven are at eye level. And that they finally have a small freezer.

◇◇◇◇◇◇◇◇◇◇◇◇◇◇◇◇◇◇◇◇◇◇◇◇◇◇◇◇◇◇◇◇◇◇◇◇◇

BEST-KEPT KITCHEN SECRET

The bin is positioned so you can just throw things in it from quite a distance. (Unfortunately it does sometimes go wrong!) And the magnetic holder for the scissors was a real find; the constant hunt for a pair of scissors is now a thing of the past.

◇◇◇◇◇◇◇◇◇◇◇◇◇◇◇◇◇◇◇◇◇◇◇◇◇◇◇◇◇◇◇◇◇◇◇◇◇

FAVORITE SURPRISING FLAVOR COMBINATIONS

Pomegranate and yogurt. And the combinations in all the dishes by the London-based chef and cookbook writer Yotam Ottolenghi. On their annual visit to the London Book Fair, Annemarieke and her business partner Claudette always try to eat at one of Ottolenghi's restaurants.

◇◇◇◇◇◇◇◇◇◇◇◇◇◇◇◇◇◇◇◇◇◇◇◇◇◇◇◇◇◇◇◇◇◇◇◇◇

FAVORITE SPICES AND HERBS

The North African spice mix ras el hanout is an absolute favorite.

◇◇◇◇◇◇◇◇◇◇◇◇◇◇◇◇◇◇◇◇◇◇◇◇◇◇◇◇◇◇◇◇◇◇◇◇◇

INSPIRATIONS

www.pinterest.com
www.marimekko.com
www.urbansandindians.com

◇◇◇◇◇◇◇◇◇◇◇◇◇◇◇◇◇◇◇◇◇◇◇◇◇◇◇◇◇◇◇◇◇◇◇◇◇

BONUS RECIPES

MY FAVORITE PICKING PLATTER

Sometimes I just love to eat some warm, crisp bread with cold cuts, cheese, fruit, and vegetables. Just put everything on a large wooden board. I call it *Plukplank*—picking platter. Ban all cutlery, eat with your hands, and forget your table manners. Just pick and mix whatever you feel like—and don't forget to lick your fingers!

These are my favorite *Plukplank* ingredients:

INGREDIENTS
BREAD (FOR EXAMPLE, A BAGUETTE CRISPED UP IN THE OVEN)
TOMATO TAPENADE
APPLES AND PEARS
MIXED GREENS
ARDENNES HAM (OR OTHER GOOD AIR-DRIED HAM)
COEUR DE CAMEMBERT AU CALVADOS (ALSO KNOWN AS CALVA D'AUGE)
VARIETY OF FRENCH CHEESES

Tip
It's also really delicious to add some asparagus tips in Ardennes ham.

PREPARATION
Preheat the oven to 400°F. Wrap a few asparagus tips in one slice of Ardennes ham (or other air-dried ham) and sprinkle with plenty of coarse sea salt and olive oil. Roast for 15 to 20 minutes.

BROCCOLI, POTATO, AND SALMON FRITTATA

SERVES 4

INGREDIENTS
4 TO 6 SMALL NEW POTATOES (ABOUT 7 OUNCES)
1 SMALL HEAD OF BROCCOLI
2 TABLESPOONS OLIVE OIL
PINCH OF SEA SALT
1 RED ONION
1 CLOVE OF GARLIC
PEPPER, TO TASTE
10.5 OUNCES SALMON, DICED
8 EGGS, BEATEN

PREPARATION
Preheat the oven to 350°F. Halve the potatoes and cut the broccoli into florets. Place in a large ovenproof pot, add just enough water to cover the potatoes and broccoli, and add the olive oil and a generous pinch of salt. Cover with a lid, place over high heat, and bring to a boil. Then turn down the heat, leaving the lid on, and continue to cook.

Meanwhile, slice the onion into rings and crush the garlic. When the potatoes are soft, add the garlic, onion, pepper to taste, salmon, and finally the eggs (the water will have evaporated by now). Cook uncovered for about 5 minutes. Then cover the pot and put in the oven for 30 minutes.

SIMPLE COCONUT SOUP

SERVES 4

INGREDIENTS
1½ CUPS FISH STOCK
2⅓ CUPS COCONUT MILK
⅔ CUP (ABOUT ⅓ POUND) SEABOB (OR REGULAR) SHRIMP
6 DRIED BAY LEAVES
7 OUNCES CHICKEN THIGHS
HANDFUL OF CILANTRO
1 RED CHILI PEPPER
3 SCALLIONS

PREPARATION
In a medium saucepan, mix the fish stock and the coconut milk. Add the shrimp and the bay leaves. Chop the remaining ingredients, including the chicken thighs, add them to the pan, and cook on low heat until the chicken is cooked through. This takes about 20 minutes.

ONE-CUP PANCAKES

SERVES 4

INGREDIENTS
1 CUP SELF-RISING FLOUR
1 CUP REDUCED-FAT MILK
1 EGG
1 APPLE, SHREDDED
PINCH OF SALT
1 TABLESPOON SUNFLOWER OIL

PREPARATION
In a medium bowl, mix all of the ingredients, except the sunflower oil, together. Heat about 1 tablespoon of sunflower oil in a frying pan over low to medium heat. Drop about ¼-cup of batter into the pan for each pancake, and cook for a few minutes or until the pancakes start to bubble on top. Then flip over and bake for another 1 to 2 minutes.

Serve with fresh fruit and honey or maple syrup.

ROASTED EGGPLANT

SERVES 4

INGREDIENTS

2 EGGPLANTS
3 TABLESPOONS OLIVE OIL, DIVIDED
SALT, TO TASTE
½-INCH PIECE FRESH GINGER
2 CLOVES OF GARLIC
1 TABLESPOON PESTO ROSSO (TOMATO PESTO)
5 TABLESPOONS HONEY
4 TEASPOONS RAS EL HANOUT

PREPARATION

Preheat the oven to 400°F. First slice and then dice the eggplant. Place the pieces in a medium-sized baking dish, sprinkle with 2 tablespoons of olive oil and salt and roast for 30 minutes.

Grate the ginger, crush the garlic, and fry in a skillet pan in 1 tablespoon of olive oil over high heat. Add the pesto, honey, and ras el hanout. Stir constantly, taking care that the mix doesn't stick to the pan. Add the eggplant and fry, adding a generous dash of olive oil in the process, until done.

Serve with couscous, pasta, or rice.

TOMATO SOUP WITH MEATBALLS

SERVES 4

INGREDIENTS

5 OUNCES TOMATO TAPENADE
14 OUNCES MINCED BEEF
1 TABLESPOON OLIVE OIL
3 14.5-OUNCE CANS OF PEELED TOMATOES
2 CLOVES OF GARLIC
½ TEASPOON CHILLI POWDER
½ TEASPOON GROUND CINNAMON
½ BUNCH PARSLEY
SALT AND PEPPER, TO TASTE

PREPARATION

In a medium bowl, mix the tapenade with the minced beef and form small balls. Heat the olive oil in a frying pan and add the meatballs. Fry them until they are browned and done. Cut the tomatoes into large chunks, mince the garlic, and add both to the pan. Add all the remaining ingredients. Stir constantly until the soup is hot; take off the heat before it boils.

Serve with bread.

MEXICAN BEAN SOUP

SERVES 4

INGREDIENTS

2 TABLESPOONS OLIVE OIL
4 CUPS PEELED AND CUBED PUMPKIN (OR BUTTERNUT SQUASH)
2 CUPS FROZEN PEAS
7 OUNCES STRING BEANS, CUT INTO 1 TO 1½-INCH PIECES
1 TABLESPOON SALT
1 15-OUNCE CAN CHILI BEANS
1 15-OUNCE CAN KIDNEY BEANS
1 15-OUNCE CAN OF BAKED BEANS IN TOMATO SAUCE
½ RED CHILI PEPPER
HANDFUL OF FRESH FLAT-LEAF PARSLEY
1¾ CUPS CANNED SWEET CORN
1 TEASPOON CHILI POWDER
1 TEASPOON CAYENNE PEPPER

PREPARATION

Pour the olive oil into a large skillet pan and place over high heat. Then add the pumpkin, peas, and string beans, along with the salt. Cover the pan and turn down the heat to medium. Cook until the pumpkin is soft (you should be able to prick it with a fork). Now add all the canned beans, including their brine and sauce. Mince the red chili pepper and the parsley and add to the pan, along with the sweet corn, chili powder, and cayenne pepper. Stir well and serve.

BANANA ICE CREAM

SERVES 4

INGREDIENTS

6 VERY RIPE BANANAS
1 TABLESPOON SMOOTH PEANUT BUTTER
1 TEASPOON COCOA POWDER

PREPARATION

Slice the bananas and place the slices side by side in large freezer bags. Freeze for 12 hours.

Blend the frozen banana slices in a food processor or blender until they resemble the consistency seen in the photo. This will necessitate brute force, but don't despair. It will be fine in the end! Add the peanut butter and the cocoa powder and blend well.

Serve in bowls.

RESOURCES

BUSINESS LISTINGS

ixxi
www.ixxidesign.com/en
Pages: 37 – 54, 75 – 96

Studio Parade
www.studioparade.nl (in Dutch only)
Pages: 37 – 54

Vintage Room
www.vintageroom.nl (in Dutch only)
Pages: 55 – 74

Bodie and Fou
www.bodieandfou.com
Pages: 97 – 112

MUSwerk
www.muswerk.nl (in Dutch only)
Pages: 113 – 130

Customr
www.customr.com
Pages: 131 – 146

wood & wool stool
www.woodwoolstool.com
Pages: 147 – 166

MaandagDaandag/Jan Rot
www.maandagdaandag.blogspot.com (in
Dutch only)
www.janrot.nl (in Dutch only)
Pages: 183 – 202

Restaurant Villa Bloemenhof
www.villabloemenhof.com (in Dutch only)
Pages: 203 – 218

Uitgeverij Snor
www.uitgeverijsnor.nl
Pages: 219 – 236, 237 – 254

FOOD BLOGS

101 Cookbooks
www.101cookbooks.com

Call Me Cupcake
www.call-me-cupcake.blogspot.com

Herriott Grace
www.herriottgrace.com

Honey & Jam
www.honeyandjam.com

Island Menu
www.islandmenu.com.au

Keke
www.youfoundkeke.com

La Tartine Gourmande
www.latartinegourmande.com

Spoon Fork Bacon
www.spoonforkbacon.com

The Forest Feast
www.theforestfeast.com

The Kitchn
www.thekitchn.com

What Katie Ate
www.whatkatieate.com

Whole Larder Love
www.wholelarderlove.com

LIFESTYLE BLOGS

Anknel and Burblets
www.anknelandburblets.com

Bright Bazaar
www.brightbazaarblog.com

Cherry Menlove
www.cherrymenlove.com

Decor8
www.decor8blog.com

Happy Interior Blog
www.happyinteriorblog.com

Junkaholique
www.junkaholique.com

Lille Lykke
www.lillelykke.blogspot.com

Little Glowing Lights
www.littleglowinglights.blogspot.com

Lobster and Swan
www.blog.lobsterandswan.com

Roost
www.roostblog.com

sf girl by bay
www.sfgirlbybay.com

Selina Lake
www.selinalake.blogspot.com

The Style Files
www.style-files.com

Zilverblauw
www.zilverblauw.nl

RETAILERS AND WHOLESALERS

Albert Heijn
www.ah.nl (in Dutch only)

Amazing Oriental
www.amazingoriental.com (in Dutch only)

Bakkerij van Heeswijk
www.bakkerijvanheeswijk.nl (in Dutch only)

Cath Kidston
www.cathkidston.com

Daylesford Organic
www.daylesford.com

Dille & Kamille
www.dille-kamille.nl (in Dutch and French only)

Divertimenti
www.divertimenti.co.uk

EkoPlaza
www.ekoplaza.nl (in Dutch only)

Fairtrade
www.fairtrade.nl (in Dutch only)

Falcon Enamelware
www.falconenamelware.com

Lakeland
www.lakeland.co.uk

Madame Charlotte
www.madame-charlotte.nl (in Dutch only)

Marks & Spencer
www.marksandspencer.eu

Melrose and Morgan
www.melroseandmorgan.com

Oldenhof
www.kookwinkel.nl (in Dutch only)

Ottomania
www.ottomania.nl

Piet Hein Eek
www.pietheineek.nl/en

Riess
www.riess.nl

Sissy-Boy
www.sissy-boy.nl (in Dutch only)

Smeg
www.smegusa.com

Steenbergs Organic
www.steenbergs.co.uk

RECICE
INDEX

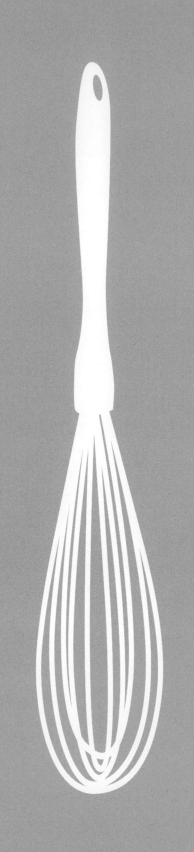

INGREDIENT INDEX

ACKNOWLEDGMENTS

Thanks to my Dutch publishers Annemarieke and Claudette, for your faith in me and my concept. Thank you to Peter Pauper Press for publishing my book in English. Thank you both for this beautiful book. And a heartfelt thank you to Mara in New York and Lisa in Utrecht.

Thank you dearest family and friends who are featured in this book. Thank you for your enthusiastic participation, the lunches, the dinners, and the gossip. I feel very privileged to be your little sister and/or friend.

Thanks Roel for the wonderful design of this book. I'm so glad that after all these years of friendship and after all our great plans and inventions we've finally made something together.

Thank you dearest blog readers; there'd be no Yvestown and no book without you. Thank you for following me on Instagram, Twitter, and Facebook. For visiting my fairs and other events. Thank you for your messages, kind words, and inspiration. Promise me that you will always say hello if you bump into me. I don't bite, only into cake.

Thanks dear Ellen Antwerp, Sophie, Monique, Ellen V., and the lovely people at the Piet Hein Eek restaurant for all your good care.

Thank you dear Mama, for all your love, patience, friendliness, and wisdom. Despite your busy life you've always taught us that it is good to get together and eat together. You've taught us that a beautifully laid table and good table manners are just as important as where your food comes from. You have taught us to respect the need for leading the life you live in a beautiful way, and for that I am ever so grateful.

Thank you my dearest Papa, how I would love to send you a copy of this book. But unfortunately one never gets a change of address if someone is saying his eternal goodbyes. I miss you. X

Thanks to my beloved Boris. I hope to be able to eat with you for many years to come.

Big kiss and lots of cake,
Yvonne

yvestown